Common Threads

Investigating and Solving School Discipline

Anthony Barber and Jeffrey G. Ulmer

ROWMAN & LITTLEFIELD EDUCATION
A division of
ROWMAN & LITTLEFIELD PUBLISHERS, INC.
Lanham • Boulder • New York • Toronto • Plymouth, UK

Published by Rowman & Littlefield Education
A division of Rowman & Littlefield
4501 Forbes Boulevard, Suite 200, Lanham, Maryland 20706
www.rowman.com

10 Thornbury Road, Plymouth PL6 7PP, United Kingdom

Copyright © 2014 by Anthony Barber and Jeffrey G. Ulmer

All rights reserved. No part of this book may be reproduced in any form or by any electronic or mechanical means, including information storage and retrieval systems, without written permission from the publisher, except by a reviewer who may quote passages in a review.

British Library Cataloguing in Publication Information Available

Library of Congress Cataloging-in-Publication Data

Barber, Anthony.
  Common threads : investigating and solving school discipline / Anthony Barber and Jeffrey G. Ulmer.
     pages cm
  Includes bibliographical references.
  ISBN 978-1-4758-0557-4 (cloth) — ISBN 978-1-4758-0558-1 (pbk.) — ISBN 978-1-4758-0559-8 (electronic) 1. School discipline. 2. Classroom management. I. Title.
  LB3012.B27 2014
  371.5—dc23   2013028535

To Denise, Brett, Braden, Bradley, and my family and friends:
thank you for your love and support. You give me hope.
—Anthony

For my wife, Rebekah. You are my world. I could never do any of
this without your support. Jake, Jolie, and Jackson,
you are my soul. I love you.
—Jeff

Contents

Disclaimer		vii
Foreword		ix
Preface		xi
Introduction		xvii
Part I	Theoretical Connections	1
	Discipline and Culture in Schools	1
	What Is the Right Behavior?	2
	Who Decides What Right Is?	3
	The Purpose of the Code	5
	Summation of Culture and Philosophies	7
	The Common Threads Model	8
Part II	Real-World Connections	11
	Pressures on Families	12
	The Ramifications of IDEA	14
	An Informed Populace: Lawyers and Lawsuits	17
	Issues of Culture and Race	19
	Focus on Safe Schools	22
	Synopsis of Key Connections	26
Part III	Practical Application	29
	Setting the Stage	29
	The Step-by-Step Process	30
	What-If Scenarios	46

	Conversations with Parents and Guardians	50
	Helpful Tips in Handling Frequent Scenarios	54
	Limitations of Common Threads	57
	Benefits of Common Threads	58
	Summation	60
Part IV	Case Studies	61
	Mutually Combative	61
	Confidential Matters	62
	Timing	63
	Just the Facts	64
	The Confession	64
	"Are You Calling My Kid a Liar?"	65
	"I Am Going to Your Boss"	66
	The Double Whack	67
	Teacher Investigation	68
	Bus Video	69
	Threat	69
	The Authority	70
	The Possible Fight	71
Scenario 1		73
Scenario 2		91
Bibliography		105

Disclaimer

This text is offered solely as a guide and potential resource for educators who live and work in a constantly changing and dynamic environment. It is not intended to be and indeed is not an all-encompassing work that addresses each and every potential situation or issue that is or may be encountered in the realm of education. It does not provide a step-by-step guaranteed manual for success via wooden application of the concepts, ideas, and suggestions presented herein. Instead, this is a rendering and distillation of information crafted by educators that may be of use to other educators. The application of that information is wholly dependent upon the innumerable facts and circumstances and other intangible components that are part and parcel of each individual challenge or opportunity that may be presented in any individual situation.

Foreword

"Investigation" is a commonly used term that is subject to any number of applications, interpretations, and definitions. Context dictates the actual meaning. As a police officer and, later, a drug agent/detective, I conducted innumerable investigations with the initial goal of determining if in fact a crime had been committed and, if so, affecting the arrest and successful prosecution of the person or persons who had engaged in the illegal activities. Now, as a lawyer, I routinely search for verification of alleged facts, and from that strive to apply established legal concepts so that I can, as an advocate, validly support and defend my client's position.

The book you are preparing to read approaches the topical definition in a distinct and different fashion than the above examples, but the foundational aspects of what an "investigation" ideally accomplishes remain consistent. It can be safely and accurately said that an investigation, irrespective of the contextual surround, is a multifaceted process of objective fact gathering, followed by a valid analysis, interpretation, and application of those facts to the individual situation.

The instant work integrates the academic, administrative, legal, and practical commonsense aspects of investigative skills within a school setting. An effective investigator, whether a detective, a lawyer, or a middle school principal, will follow the path of reliable information to a valid and supportable end determination. As this book makes clear, the process is not one in which speculation or innuendo come into play.

Common Threads: Investigating and Solving School Discipline is a must-have inclusion to the professional library of any contemporary educator desirous of meeting today's ever-changing academic challenges and demands.

Michael J. Hawley, BS, MPA, JD

Preface

As a new assistant principal, I can remember processing my first disciplinary issue. Margie (fictitious) received a discipline referral for being disrespectful to a peer. I can recall reading the referral, chatting with the teacher who wrote it, and feeling pretty good about what I thought had happened. Margie, who had been in the office quite a bit last year (so I had been told), apparently slammed her books on her desk and yelled "Shut up!" to a girl who sat directly beside her. Simple enough. I looked at the discipline and realized the code would call for an administrative detention for being disrespectful. Again, the process seemed pretty straightforward—that was until I actually chatted with Margie.

As one can imagine, Margie did not see the story quite the way the others did. In fact, there were several points that did not match the previous ones. First, Margie did not bring any books into class that day. In fact, she stated that what the teacher heard was her foot as it got caught under the desk. She also stated that she was getting tired of hearing a girl talking to her friends during class. She was merely trying to get the other students to be quiet. In addition, she stated that the teacher was working with a student on the other side of the room when the event took place and that he took the word of the other students over hers.

As Margie continued to chat, I feverously took notes and began to recognize that this simple disciplinary issue was not going to be as straightforward as I had anticipated. I realized that in spite of my formal education and the plethora of learned theories concerning human behavior, social interactions, and instructional leadership, I was never formally taught a systemic process for handling disciplinary issues. Did one even exist?

I can recall university professors skimming the topic of discipline by saying, "Use your best judgment, and follow the discipline code." Until that day with Margie, I just assumed that sound advice would be enough. However, sloganistic statements only go so far when reality knocks and interpretation begins. I realized that without a plan, I was lost in the translation of trying to deduce these social interactions without even a starting point.

Once that happened, all of my previous moves came into question. Should I have chatted with the teacher first? Should I have brought the two girls in together? What questions should I have asked? Was I assuming truth too early? Did my knowing that Margie had been in the office before cloud my judgment? The magnitude of this outcome resided in my hands. It was my move, and people were waiting.

In current times, educators have placed a tremendous emphasis on making data-driven decisions. In fact, it is hard to comprehend the enormity of data that is available to us concerning student achievement, budget issues, discipline, and so forth. However, despite being able to access all of this data (specifically the discipline data), we have yet to create a systematic procedure for attaining facts prior to reviewing our discipline data, which calls into question the validity of the original numbers.

To all critical researchers, the process of attaining the results is just as crucial, if not more so, than the results themselves. Without the ability to replicate a particular procedure (standardized), our practice can cause questions concerning the information's relevance and reliability. Stemming from that fateful day with Margie, the necessity to formalize an investigative method for schools was apparent and warranted to ensure that each child is afforded the right to a consistent and valid process.

Sometimes, the most simple of ideas can be the most difficult to execute. We think to ourselves, *How did I ever miss that?* only to be reminded that trial and error in education never ceases. For example, consider making pumpkin pie. The first step in the process is to gather the ingredients. Next, by following the directions and specific cooking measurements and requirements, one can attain the proper outcome (the pie) and be able to plan serving specifics.

PREFACE xiii

Ingredients "What?"	Directions "How?"	Outcome "Desired effect"
Pumpkin, sugar, . . .	Take two teaspoons . . .	How to serve it (whipped cream, with coffee, etc.)

Obviously, this example serves as a metaphor for our understanding the complexity of school discipline and the current situation. Most schools have a discipline code; additionally, most schools have a set of consequences that can be assigned after an infraction to the discipline code occurs. Yet the most important part of the process is missing.

Ingredients "What?"	Directions "How?"	Outcome "Desired effect"
Pumpkin, sugar . . .	**Guesstimate**	Unknown

What would happen to our pie if we neglected the directions? No matter how much coffee was served, it would be difficult to judge the reaction of the eaters when so much of the process was left to chance.

Now, consider school discipline. For example, a warning could be given to a student who forgets to take off his or her hat in school. Furthermore, if the student continues to wear a hat, perhaps a detention might be warranted. Yet, the most important part of the entire process remains undefined. How can administrators determine what consequence should sustain if they cannot identify how the conclusion was made?

Discipline code "What behaviors?"	Investigative methods "How to"	Consequence "Possible outcomes"
Wearing a hat in school	**CURRENT VOID**	First offense: Warning Second offense: Detention

Imagine if your son or daughter was being accused of wearing a hat in school. Although not the end of the world, no one enjoys negative news from school. Chances are, you would want to know the facts of the accusation, especially if your son or daughter happened to deny the incident. Consider greater impacts of discipline such as bullying or harassment that bring larger consequences.

Although the district attempts to garner the appearance of consistency (using a code), administrators cannot truly defend that claim by not being able to verbalize and replicate the structure of investigation. Knowing the methodology helps inform the value judgment of the outcome.

Repetition is the key to standardization and success. Think about a Big Mac. No matter what country, a Big Mac tastes like a Big Mac. Much like a franchise, educators must establish a recognizable protocol for investigation to build understanding and support for its product (the outcome of the investigation).

Discipline issues in schools involve human reaction. The emotional stress that comes with the judgment of one's behavior speaks to our ability to hurt or heal with our words and actions. Again, the purpose of school discipline is to assist students in becoming the best they can possibly be while also respecting the rights of others. It is a delicate balance and one that necessitates clear direction on the part of administrators to deliver the correct amount of guidance. Needless to say, being an administrator is not an easy job.

There have been numerous texts that have attempted to assist administrators, such as Chad Mason's *Assistant Principal's Guide . . . Into the Fire* or Paul Smith's *What Do You Do Around Here Anyway?*[1] These manuscripts are excellent resources for current and future administrators when it comes to school discipline and a host of other topics. However, until the educational community recognizes the void in the investigation process and looks to implement a consistent system, student outcomes will be left to the will and whim of each individual principal.

During the past two decades, both Jeff and I have processed thousands of referrals. Over the course of our tenure, we have been able to use the system and hone in on improvements through experience. It is our hope that upon reviewing this text, the reader will be better prepared to handle investigations in schools than ever before. We wish you all the best.

NOTE

1. Chad Mason, *An Assistant Principal's Guide . . . Into the Fire: How to Prepare for and Survive the Position* (Lanham, MD: Rowman & Littlefield, 2007); Paul R. Smith, *What Do You Do Around Here Anyway? Real-Life Discussion Generators for Wannabe Principals* (Lanham, MD: Hamilton Books, 2010).

Introduction

Common Threads: Investigating and Solving School Discipline is a practical, effective, and easy-to-implement system of how to conduct investigations for school administrators. By separating fact from hearsay and organizing information into discernible categories, investigative strategies are streamlined to increase the efficiency and gravity of interpretations and results.

Common Threads is organized into four well-synthesized sections that read like a straightforward handbook, free of superfluous jargon or "eduspeak." Beginning with a section on the theory behind the practice, *Common Threads* takes a look at the history and rationale behind school-based investigations and the collective struggles that administrators have to endure during the investigative process, whether it be disciplinary situations, student-to-student entanglements, or other building-based issues that require any sort of investigation.

In the second part, *Common Threads* analyzes the real-world situations that are impacting today's administrators when it comes to investigation in schools. Focus of this section revolves around family structures, cultural differences, safe-school efforts, and legal ramifications that affect schools' personnel on a daily basis. *Common Threads* attempts to connect these pressing issues with a clear rationale for why an investigative methodology is warranted.

Common Threads continues in the third part with a practical step-by-step guide to conducting and orchestrating the investigative process that will ensure clear results based on the collection and association of facts and truths. This well-defined and sequential section will spell out exactly how to create, carry out, and complete an effective investigative process, ending with how to present your findings to students, parents, fellow administrators, and colleagues. The inclusion of sample charts and text adds to the simplistic and thorough explanations of the methodology.

Common Threads adds realistic, timely, and comprehensive case studies in the last section, where the reader can see the system put into action. The how-to aspect of *Common Threads* is put to the test with many what-if situations that are designed to challenge, reassure, and inspire administrators to put their faith and confidence into the methodology and process.

Written by two current school administrators, *Common Threads* lives and breathes in schools in the here and now. Its merits have been refined and perfected on the job by field testing its processes and resolutions with every new investigative opportunity the authors experienced with true-to-life situations and incidents. *Common Threads* not only streamlines the investigative process; it creates a cornerstone of communication, reliability, and accuracy that will help schools thrive and grow in an ever-changing educational climate.

1

THEORETICAL CONNECTIONS

DISCIPLINE AND CULTURE IN SCHOOLS

Schools are a reflection of society, in that they represent the need to balance the rights of the individual with the rights of the collective. Citizens within the society must define guidelines for acceptable social behavior in order to maintain social order. Schools, on a smaller scale, are mini-societies, and thus also have the charge to balance individual and group needs. Inherent in this design is the necessity to define what the "acceptable" level of social behavior represents to all stakeholders who exist in the organization. We call the attempt to maintain social order the discipline code.

A discipline code, or any code for acceptable social behavior, attempts to express the agreed-upon conduct for students within the school. A code defines acceptable interactions. These interactions are what make up the customs and manners by which people act together within a given social order.[1] However, to truly understand and appreciate these exchanges, one must first become acquainted with the presence of culture and its impact on our daily lives.

Culture is the inner workings of people, their interactions and interdependence as a functioning society.[2] It is this culture that establishes our actions within this school system. When analyzing behavior, one possible explanation may reside within the work of Edward T. Hall and his levels of culture. Hall feels that culture exists on three separate levels: technical, formal, and informal.[3] For the purpose of our discussions, we will focus upon formal culture.

Formal culture, according to Hall, has to do with what is "proper or improper" behavior, which for our purposes, signifies the type of behavior we would locate in a school's discipline code. The code defines an agreed-upon set of standards that maintain order so that the educational process can exist. For example, although wearing a hat may be socially acceptable at the mall, the act of wearing a hat has been deemed as unacceptable behavior in the school setting because hats can disrupt the educational process. Now, whether we personally agree with this premise or not, if a school has established a formal culture that hats are unacceptable, the "right" response for students would be not to wear one. Failure to adhere to the formal culture could place a student in jeopardy of the consequences of the code.

In addition, "The formal level of culture is tied up to feelings and is very resistant to change."[4] Once a formal culture has been established as a rule, people will have a more difficult time accepting variations. For instance, if students are not permitted to chew gum and someone suggests the brain research behind why gum chewing should be allowed, people are more likely to (at first) support the no-gum-chewing policy because it is the rule. In understanding this aspect of formal culture, and knowing that society is ever changing, formal culture presents problems when it comes to interpretation by individuals.

WHAT IS THE RIGHT BEHAVIOR?

Schools are established with purpose. Recall the views of the Puritans on children. If children were born sinners, schools must be set up to correct this precondition.[5] Throughout the history of education, the determination of "sacred" information guides the fortitude of need. Although not driven by the same fundamental structure as our earlier settlers, today's schools endorse what the people have determined as mission critical.

What complicates the structure of determining what right is and who makes that decision has to do with the pluralistic nature of today's school environments. Different belief structures vie for their position within the framework of what is right. Assumptions of consensus are damaged the more diverse a population's thinking is permitted to be.

For example, in a Catholic school, those that do not believe in God would not necessarily be welcome. If there were behavioral expectations that were not being followed, such as kneeling for a specific religious event, chances are the leadership of the school would ask that student to conform or leave.

Modern, free schools service various sects of people. The expansion of the system provides for more differences to coexist. In other words, the more voices we add to the mix, the more those voices want to be heard and appreciated. What people believe the purpose of school to be dictates the type of school one will have and the details for its governance.

Behavior depends on the social context and who is judging it. For instance, calling out would have been a reprehensible act in 1635 in a Latin grammar school; however, in today's classroom settings, there are times when this type of behavior is permitted. The reason resides in the social context and the judge of the behavior.

Betsy Gunzelmann, in her book entitled *Hidden Dangers: Subtle Signs of Failing Schools*, speaks to the idea of challenging assumptions, beliefs, and practice when it comes to today's schools.[6] Successful organizations examine the items that have traditionally been unspeakable. The pluralistic nature of today's schools happens to be one of those hidden factors that expedite the need to define behavior. But whose behavior matters more?

WHO DECIDES WHAT RIGHT IS?

Public systems develop strategic plans to define the vision and mission of the school districts. These plans are created with the assurance of various stakeholders found within the community. The work of these individuals creates the overarching ideals for schools to function. It is the right of the community to elect officials to a school board to establish the school system, and it is the duty of the school board to secure the personnel to carry out the desires of the community, so long as the educational laws are being followed.

The function of the school delineates between the policies and regulations. For example, school boards are charged with creating policy for the district to follow. However, policy can be very difficult to "follow" because of the nature by which it is created.

What creates the functionality of the policy are the regulations (or guidelines) that accompany it. For example, a district may have a policy on attendance (e.g., school is mandatory); however, what constitutes the "breakage of the policy" may be identified through the guidelines (e.g., vacations during state testing will be marked as unexcused). As noted by Seamus Boyce, school administrators need to be clear when it comes to the separation and delineation between policy and regulations to ensure safety and less liability.[7]

Revisiting Gunzelmann, another hidden component to the system resides in the fact that although stakeholders (many views) make policy, most times, administrators (a select group) make the regulations and the call when it comes to the interpretation.[8] Although necessary to operationalize the organization (get things done), the downside to this necessity creates a level of discretion on the part of the administration.

When we investigate peoples' dissatisfaction with school discipline, we tend to find key themes such as lack of consistency and actions occurring or not occurring based upon how the "disciplinary" interprets the events.[9] Owen Webb examined the idea of discretion in his study "Student Perceptions of Discretion in Discipline: Seeking Resolution and Restoration in a Punitive Culture."[10] Discretion is the capacity to make an informed decision on a situation as it relates to the decision maker's authority and his or her ability to consider various factors.[11] One study concludes that there is a "need for a community vision for discipline" in order to create a trustworthy environment.[12]

Perhaps here resides a subtle crack found within the system. Although the discipline code is transparent (black and white), both the individuals involved in a discipline situation and the individual charged with administering the event must use discretion and opinion.

Many would argue that one of the charges of the public school is to build capacity for citizenship. Doyle Stevick and Bradley Levinson in *Reimagining Civic Education: How Diverse Societies Form Democratic Citizens* recount the notion of branding usable tenets in an ever-changing environment to sustain the debate that "one size does not it all."[13] For example, although we realize certain drivers can proceed faster and safer than others, this does not mean that the practicality of having individual speed limits can or should exist. As one could imagine, even though that may be a wonderful idea, the task would be too great to administer.

As the population grows, so too does the governance of action to accomplish work. Within this framework, the rights of the individuals and the collective are protected by limiting freedoms. The speed limit reflects a discipline code in a school system by establishing the proper behavior for the situation. The consequences of the outcome (a ticket, warning, etc.) are established by the police officer after the investigation has occurred. The necessity to have both a code and consequences along with a methodology for investigation is warranted to address a system that serves many individuals.

THE PURPOSE OF THE CODE

The reason school systems rely on discipline codes resides in their members and their individuality. Within this bombardment of varying perspectives comes the necessity to create a standard, a guide to which all members can adhere. But where does our basis for such a standard exist? Perhaps the work of Walther Feinberg and Jonas Soltis can assist with this question.[14]

Feinberg and Soltis identified three views of a school that can shed some light on our discussion concerning the origins of discipline and our philosophy of schooling. To Feinberg and Soltis, some people believe schools exist to teach students how to function in a given society. Feinberg and Soltis defined this belief as functionalism. Under a functionalist view, schools look to fulfill the needs of the society by preparing students to contribute to it. Schools replicate the aspects of the society, so that the society can continue and flourish. Inherent in this philosophy is a need to "standardize" the behaviors of the individuals in order to place the collective (the society) higher than the individual.

Discipline codes are functional in nature in that the same set of behaviors is expected by all individuals. Despite the multiple perspectives and experiences of our students, the code is impartial to individual positions. In a sense, fair is equal, and the set standard of discipline cannot exist if left to the interpretation of varying perspectives. There is one code, one set of behaviors that are acceptable, and any deviation from these behaviors would be seen as a violation of the code (subject to disciplinary action). A functionalist would always follow the discipline code, without exception, because failure to do so would create an imbalance to the system itself and would be seen as unjust.

The second philosophy that Feinberg and Soltis identified was that held by conflict theorists. Conflict theorists believe that schools are in existence to maintain the social power of the dominant class. They see the replication of the prevailing social class norms as purposeful and harmful to individuals who do not make up the dominant class. Fair, for a conflict theorist, is not equal because one size does not fit all. A discipline code, for example, does not account for one's economic, social, ethnic, or family background. To a conflict theorist, there may be special circumstances in one's background that would make the discipline code prejudiced against the individual who does not "fit" into the dominant class.

A conflict theorist would tend to struggle with one specific disciplinary code. A conflict theorist may use past experiences or background information in order to "justify" the deviation from following the code in a lockstep manner. A conflict theorist would not worry about disrupting the system that a code looks to establish because the standard is already flawed (suppresses individuals or groups not found within the majority of power).

The last philosophy of Feinberg and Soltis is "interpretivism." Within this philosophy, schools are not seen as having a "planned" purpose either to replicate a given society (functionalism) or to keep members of a society from attaining equity (conflict theory). Under an interpretive view, schools are more local in that they serve to respond to the needs of a community surrounding the school. Within this philosophy, fair depends on the situation and the circumstances surrounding it. An interpretive person handling discipline would not be concerned with maintaining social order to righting social injustice but would only be concerned with doing "what is needed" for the given situation and the people involved.

SUMMATION OF CULTURE AND PHILOSOPHIES

When taking into account culture and the philosophies of schools, one can begin to build a picture of the origin of our discipline codes, why they were established, and how they might be interpreted based upon our beliefs. As administrators, our goal is to make every effort to do our best to assist a child to succeed. Within this maxim, the responsibility for action usually resides within our decisions. However, can we even begin to judge situations without first securing the facts?

One of the greatest challenges we face as school personnel is the necessity to suppress our personal agendas (philosophies) prior to handling any type of investigative procedure. Doing the right thing is easy, but agreeing on the right thing becomes a daunting task for educated people who possess different philosophies and procedures. An administrator has the dual responsibility to be both the investigator and the judge (setting consequences). One would hope that we would be able to take a clear approach when handling the issues of proper and improper behavior. However, without a formal system for investigating, we are left with only our own philosophy and a myriad of questions as it pertains to what is right. Whether we believe in a functionalist, conflict theorist, or interpretive viewpoint, the necessity to secure the facts in a systematic way must be at the forefront of every investigation to sustain accuracy for each particular instance.

Communication is paramount in almost any situation of success, and discipline is no exception. Without a formal system, conversations suffer, and we are left to struggle to find the words to explain ourselves and the process we utilized to all stakeholders. For example, how many times have administrators been asked to explain the discipline process that was followed to parents, teachers, students, and central office personnel only to have it questioned by a lack of common understanding? As these questions persist, it might become easy to assume that people are questioning the administrator's competence rather than reacting to our lack of common understanding and an ability to express ourselves to the given situation.

Without formalizing a constant approach for all administrators, individual rationalizations hinder our ability to gain trust and support for our decisions. And this lack of trust places us into situations that call into question our practice. Education is a people business, and without open communication, our efforts to assist each and every child will not be sustained.

THE COMMON THREADS MODEL

Research is the prime ingredient in sustaining usable processes. The common threads model utilizes the qualitative researcher process to shape its foundation by providing a conceptual framework for investigations. In fact, the common threads model is the essence of qualitative research and holds true to the tenets that establish its legitimacy.

Sharan Merriam states that "qualitative researchers are interested in understanding meaning people have constructed, that is, how they make sense of their experiences."[15] Within this statement lies the essence of qualitative research and our practice as educational investigators. In each instance of discipline, some type of action (written, spoken, or physical) has occurred. The administrator's task is to define the experience of the action through the lens of the individuals who were involved.

Although the work of defining one's experience may seem complex, the actual day-to-day responsibilities play out in a very simplified manner. For example, as a school official, disciplinary issues are usually reported to us by other parties. Principals try to discover what happened so that they can address the situation with an appropriate response. Here is where they become qualitative researchers.

In qualitative research, the researcher is the primary instrument in gathering data concerning how people lived through and what they felt about their experiences in a given situation.[16] In most instances, the administrators are not present for the action and therefore must rely on qualitative techniques to attain information in order to create a reasonable assessment of what occurred. As John Creswell states, qualitative research can take the form of interviews, observations, audio/video data, text and image analysis, and document analysis.[17]

One of the greatest aspects to any research has to do with the validity (legitimacy) of the investigative information. In order to build an authentic case, the qualitative researcher must be able to evaluate various forms of data to locate the patterns within it. One can accomplish this task by utilizing member checks for responses, plentiful descriptions of events, and triangulation (analyzing various points of data to locate consistencies within it) of all data. Once completed, the researcher will have the opportunity to identify a plausible framework to build reasonable conclusions.

The common threads method holds fast to the principles of qualitative research. By evaluating individuals and written interpretations of events, the administrator develops a rich text surrounding each account of the action. Triangulation occurs by evaluating each interpretation as a collective while also taking into account other related data sources (audio tapes, images, etc.).

In addition to the format for inquiry, the common threads method follows a qualitative protocol for questioning. In qualitative research, how and why responses guide the researcher's inquiries to create meaning in context beyond literal interpretations.[18] As statements are reported, member checks (interview questioning techniques) guide the administrator's ability to get to the reasons behind the event in order to create a context for what happened and for future planning.

The legitimacy of the common threads method is present within the rules for qualitative research. Crafted over various universities and years of trial and error, the foundation for qualitative data collection lies within the process and its people. It is the replication of best practice research that supplies the researcher with the best attempt to secure truth while minimizing bias.

As one enters into the next section of this text, one will be introduced to the practical application and systematic use for the common threads model. Hopefully, by taking into account the theory and practical application to this system, we will be able to build a shared confidence in our ability to investigate incidents in our schools with consistency and accuracy.

NOTES

1. Gary K. Claubaugh and Edward G. Rozycki, *Understanding Schools: The Foundations of Education* (New York: Harper & Row, 1990).
2. Claubaugh and Rozycki, *Understanding Schools*.

3. Edward T. Hall, *The Silent Language* (Greenwich, CT: Fawcett, 1959).

4. Claubaugh and Rozycki, *Understanding Schools*, 128.

5. William Jeynes, *American Educational History: School, Society, and the Common Good* (Thousand Oaks, CA: Sage, 2007).

6. Betsy Gunzelmann, *Hidden Dangers: Subtle Signs of Failing Schools* (Lanham, MD: Rowman & Littlefield, 2007).

7. Seamus P. Boyce, "Inadvertent Board Actions That Create Liability," *School Administrator* 66, no. 4 (2009): 34.

8. Gunzelmann, *Hidden Dangers*.

9. Daniel M. Besaw, "An Investigation into School-wide Discipline Policies" (PhD diss., Pacific Lutheran University, Tacoma, WA, 2006).

10. Owen D. Webb, "Student Perceptions of Discretion in Discipline: Seeking Resolution and Restoration in a Punitive Culture" (Master's thesis, Brock University, St. Catharines, Ontario, 2009).

11. Martha S. Feldman, *Social Limits to Discretion: An Organizational Perspective* (Oxford: Oxford University Press, 1992).

12. M. Jaeger, "The Use of Discretionary Authority: The Safe Schools Act, 2000, and the Faculty of St. Roy's Catholic Secondary School" (paper, Brock University, St. Catharines, Ontario, 2005).

13. E. Doyle Stevick and Bradley A. U. Levinson, *Reimagining Civic Education: How Diverse Societies Form Democratic Citizens* (Lanham, MD: Rowman & Littlefield, 2007).

14. Walter Feinberg and Jonas F. Soltis, *School and Society* (New York: Teachers College Press, 1998).

15. Sharan B. Merriam, *Qualitative Research and Case Study Application in Education* (San Francisco: Jossey-Bass, 1998).

16. Robert R. Sherman and Rodman B. Webb, *Qualitative Research in Education: Focus and Methods* (London: Falmer, 1988).

17. W. John Creswell, *Research Design: Qualitative, Quantitative and Mixed Methods Approaches*, 2nd ed. (Thousand Oaks, CA: Sage, 2003).

18. Robert K. Yin, *Case Study Research: Design and Methods*, 2nd ed. (Thousand Oaks, CA: Sage, 1994).

REAL-WORLD CONNECTIONS

In today's fast-paced environment, some may question the necessity for a systematic investigation structure. There are many administrators that have been "doing discipline for years" without a formal system. Why would they need to change now?

In the educational realm, contentment and sarcasm sometimes prevent exploration; today's successes do not always breed victory for the future. Effective organizations foster opportunities to be introspective. In this manner, change comes by design (proper planning and foresight into the future) instead of by crisis (reaction to crisis). Labeled as strategic planning, the processes by which leaders rededicate themselves to the mission by way of the data produce valuable inquiry. These conversations bridge the gap between what is and what could be.

The current landscape in education is constantly shifting, calling for school districts to change or succumb to mediocrity. Today's schools must examine their investigative methods to remain current. Failure to do so could cause serious gaps when it comes to the fidelity of disciplinary practice. Like fractures in a levy, if left unattended over time, these cracks will result in significant implications for our school personnel.

Identified are five major shifts taking place in education that are causing school personnel to examine their investigative practice. Obviously, there are other actions that are impacting disciplinary practice; however, these identified themes appear to have a tremendous influence on investigations.

PRESSURES ON FAMILIES

Why do people become so distressed when it comes to instances of discipline? Perhaps this answer is positioned within our passions as human beings. Discipline involves emotion. Consider the phone calls principals make to parents and guardians concerning disciplinary issues. These conversations are often met with emotional responses. Parents may sometimes feel administrators are calling their parenting skill into question or perhaps questioning the integrity of their child. Although best intentioned, honest efforts can sometimes be misinterpreted.

Perhaps one could state that a positive relationship must first be established with families prior to ever making a discipline call. True. Few could argue that a friendly first contact would make all the difference. Yet, in today's demanding world, it may be difficult to make those personal connections prior to incidents occurring in our schools. Although not an excuse, time is of the essence for school personnel during the course of any given day.

Current society places tremendous pressure on families. The pressure causes uneasiness that is sometimes represented in our personal interactions with people. First, consider our economy. In being a capitalist state, our economic hopes and dreams rest solely on the hinges of supply and demand. As other nations continue to enter both the global and U.S. market, pressure builds on our country to produce or perish.

In addition, rising health-care cost, social security issues, and affordability of basic needs continue to influence the emotional state of our nation's people. These pressures play a significant role in our communities' feelings concerning its families and their ability to maintain a basic standard of living, all of which extend to our interactions with people both in and out of the school system.

We are also witnessing the rise of the single family and extended home situations.[1] Addressing the house, the job, and the bills is taxing enough, but when we add securing a successful future for his or her children to the mix of a single parent, the tasks may appear daunting. In the words of former president George W. Bush, being a single mother with two children is "the toughest job in America."

What compounds the issue with families and school personnel has to do with conflict and conflict avoidance. Julia Richardson, in "Avoidance as an Active Mode of Conflict Resolution," states that "avoidance is a powerful weapon against the wellbeing of an organization."[2] When factions disagree, there are various methods utilized to build consensus. However, political correctness or sheer conscious avoidance sometimes thwarts the efforts by ending conversations when they should begin.

Principals across the globe enter into uncomfortable conversations all the time. Our desire to "fix" the problem may be the problem itself. Often people want to start with solutions instead of first determining what happened. Likewise, folks sometimes jump to the conclusion prior to establishing the root cause.

For example, suppose a principal had two students who were not getting along. In a conflict-mediation model, perhaps allowing the two students to come together in dialogue would be a logical outcome. However, the outcome cannot take precedent prior to the investigation. Although good intentioned, jumping to the conclusion before the facts can have serious consequences for all parties involved.

Conflict is a necessary component to progress. Its avoidance only serves to foster contempt for change, which can create hostility toward those who are subjected to the "non-action." Furthermore, the developmental needs of students must be addressed as we consider investigations, school discipline, and curiosity. As students become more aware, their inquisitive nature starts to blossom. Even in discipline situations, children want to understand why things have occurred, and it is the school's responsibility to teach them.

Some administrators view this questioning as a form of disrespect. However, all are entitled to a nonbiased investigation. It is the administrator's failure to identify and verbalize the process taken to solicit the facts that causes the initial breakdown. Yet, for too long, we have had no process to share. And therefore, the explanations appear haphazard or coerced.

Furthermore, there are administrators who look to negotiate every instance of school discipline. Either too busy or well intentioned, their "let's make a deal" attitude creates divisions for staff and students. Not knowing where the administrator stands from one issue to the next and lacking a consistent process creates mistrust and eventually avoidance on the part of staff members. This practice breaks down the fabric of school culture by creating perceived "favorites."

Another problem that hinders conversation is the choice of language principals use with students and families. "Eduspeak" has been labeled as jargon that educators use when communicating professional components of the job to noneducators.[3] Avoidance from families certainly can be attributed to fear of conflict. Yet, educators must also consider the language that we utilize when communicating with families and students, particularly about emotional circumstances such as discipline. Without common language, relationships diminish, leaving our families no choice but to fill in the gaps for themselves.

The rank of the administrator has also changed over time. The days of "because I said so" does not hold as much weight as before. When disagreement occurs, "explanation by rank" does not lend itself to cultivating lasting relationships. Administrators can garner more trust from families by taking the time to explain decisions. With a proper system, we will have the ability to use power (the details of the system) rather than our rank to communicate a position.

Be it a fluctuating economy, changing family structures, or any other factor occurring outside the school, the goal when handling investigations and discipline is to ensure that children are treated justly. Administrators need to focus on behavior, not the child. And they need to do it without the association of guilt that can often be placed on families that are already burdened.

School personnel have the opportunity to assist with these situations. One of the best ways administrators can foster consistency is through a stable investigation method. As the pressures of today's world mount for individual situations, perhaps having a consistent approach to investigating will make our communications with families more congenial and clearly defined.

THE RAMIFICATIONS OF IDEA

Since its inception in 1975, Public Law 94-142, the Individuals with Disabilities Education Act (IDEA), has created both positive opportunities along with difficult challenges for educators across this country.

The initial premise behind the act encompasses the moral imperative to do what is necessary to support all students in the least restrictive environment. Throughout the last several decades, school administrators have had to make adaptations to existing educational practices to not only fulfill the legal requirements of the law, but also ensure an equal playing field for all.[4]

The number of students who are involved in special education has grown to over 12 percent.[5] To this idea, administrators are almost guaranteed to have some sort of special education situation on a daily basis. Within this premise, the need to be solid in one's practice and procedures in special education is not only a nicety, but also a necessity.

However, it seems like new policy and procedures are created yearly to continually modify the act to ensure its effectiveness. As response-to-intervention and prereferral teams continue to examine individual student needs within the framework of the educational environment, so too will administrators need to stay abreast of current educational practices that are legally and ethically sound.

When dealing with disciplinary issues and special education students or even ones believed to be special education eligible (Child Find Law), it is imperative to utilize data to not only determine what has occurred but also see if the demonstrated behavior can be attributed to the child's disability. Within the realm of functional behavior assessments and behavior support plans, administrators must constantly be able to understand the social interactions of children as they relate to their disability. "Tweaking an Individualized Education Program (IEP)" is only as effective as the data that supports the suggested change, especially when it comes to behavior.

In addition to the needs of the child, in the more recent past, the audience of a special education child is expanding. Advocates and specialty personnel are in regular attendance at IEP meetings along with family members. In addition, mediations, due process hearings, and settlements are all part of a district's reality. As these practices continue to increase, school personnel will need to be sound in their data and investigative practice.

The question of special education and rights has much to do with culture as well as the law. Recall Edward Hall's levels of culture. Much of the special education law attempts to guarantee that the "correct" approach to student rights is taken when dealing with a special education student. However, educators know that being perfect may not always be right for a given situation. Here is where the difficulty resides. How does one follow the law perfectly but also provide for the social structure of student life and behavior patterns?

Much like a discipline handbook, special education law sets forth a premise for technical culture (how to get things done). However, without a clearly objective system of investigation, each individual administrator is left to decipher his or her impressions of reality, a practice surely not envisioned by proponents of IDEA, thus leaving the administrators to defend their methods solely based on what they believe to be best practice.

For example, prior to major consequences being levied to a special education student, there are often times when administrators must go through a manifestation determination to decide if the behavior exhibited was due to the child's disability or not. However, according to Antonis Katsiyannis, "There are no empirically validated methods to make a determination as to whether or not misbehavior was related to a disability."[6] With the lack of a centralized system, determination hearings could be considered nothing more than discussion of the child's disabilities as they relate to the specifics of the event in question.

If this previous scenario was true, one could argue that the recording of the specific events then becomes one of the prime factors for determining whether or not a child's behavior is within his or her control (along with the habitual nature of the student's prior behaviors and outcomes of the events). At this point, the IEP team assumes the role of lawyer, judge, and jury.

The latter is not meant to be an assault on the process utilized by schools to adhere to the mandate. Best practice would stipulate having meaningful discussion with all parties prior to assigning consequences for IEP students (for all students for that matter). Yet, the paradox to the special education system must be addressed—how can there be mandate after mandate for administrators to follow after the data has been secured for decisions but no system for collecting the data prior to manifestation decisions?

The irony lies within the very nature of discretion and the law. In a system (special education) that attempts to level the playing field for all students, the lack of discretion on the back end of special education discipline issues provides a greater degree of discretion on the front end of the data collection, thus creating an imbalance to a system that forces balance. To truly balance the system, a standardize methodology must reside on both sides of the pendulum prior to and directly after an incident occurs to ensure equality and eliminate bias.

Special education is a constant topic of school reform, especially when it comes to school discipline. Utilization of a consistent approach to investigation could limit some of the misconceptions parents have of our process and strengthen administrators' ability to be legally defendable.

AN INFORMED POPULACE: LAWYERS AND LAWSUITS

In today's litigious society, the ability to maintain consistency in protocol is critical to the success of the school district. Around every corner, there are those waiting to lunge at the opportunity to hold the school accountable for an error in protocol. One does not have to search very long to encounter someone that has either been named in a lawsuit or testified in a due process hearing to know that being accurate and thorough are mainstays in the legal system.

There are over sixty-six thousand entries in Proquest (dissertation website) when the key terms "schools and lawsuits" are searched. Many of these suits cite breaches in protocol as a main problem. These breaches are mostly associated with value judgments—personal decisions often identified as negligent practices.

For example, an assistant principal was requested to testify in an expulsion hearing concerning a student's exclusion from school. (The student was accused of continually harassing another student.) When the incident occurred, the assistant principal "investigated" the situation and felt confident that the student did indeed commit this act, as the student admitted to the action. He suspended the child and held fast that the student received an accurate punishment.

The parents of the child hired an attorney and proceeded to the hearing. The assistant principal was asked to produce evidence that led him to this conclusion. Although he did indeed interview the students in question (the accused and accuser), he did not secure other testimony from the surrounding students. In fact, he did not feel that was necessary, as he believed he had an admission at the time of the incident. (Note: The school's attorney also believed that an admission of guilt on the part of the defendant was sufficient to prove the assistant principal was just in administering a consequence for the action.)

The defendant's attorney did have the opportunity to question bystanders and painted a very different picture. When questioned, the defendant explained that he was "intimidated" by the assistant principal, which led to his admission of guilt. Without the other witnesses' statements or the ability to produce a standardized method that is utilized on a daily basis, the school was left to embrace the case on a recanted admission. The school board, having no evidence to dispel the accusation of intimidation, was directed to overturn the suspension and agreed to pay the attorney's fees for the student.

Situations like this one are unfortunately becoming the norm. Enormous settlements are being paid to families. Sometimes they are justified, but other times are the result of the inability to produce proper procedure and consistency in our practice. Whether we agree with the idea that "anyone can sue for any reason," perfect practice with proactive measures outweighs procrastination and conjecture.

Perhaps the complexity of the system has created the need for expert assistance. The fabric of trust with school personnel wanes with each new catastrophe reported by the news outlets. In addition, the ever-changing laws compound interpretation and provide for more instances of confusion and mistrust.

Alexander Wiseman, in *Principals under Pressure: The Growing Crisis*, captures a key component to the pressure on principals by asking leaders to examine the "managerial activity of principals" along with the policy.[7] Wiseman understands that as the complexity of a principal's job mounts, so too does the need for assistance become critically important. Leadership in a vacuum generates dysfunction and confusion for those on the outside of prudence.

Robert Marzano, in *What Works in Schools*, identifies the need for schools to focus upon building safe and orderly environments. Although this research rightfully belongs in the safe schools section of this text, it also speaks to the litigious nature of our current practice. Establishing clear school-wide rules and procedures for student behavior and assigning the appropriate stated consequences for said behaviors creates a more sustainable, safer school, and it also minimizes personal bias by making expectations overt.[8]

The next step in this process is to establish and publish the methodology associated with attaining the information between knowing the rule and assigning the consequence. Within this gap lies the missing component.

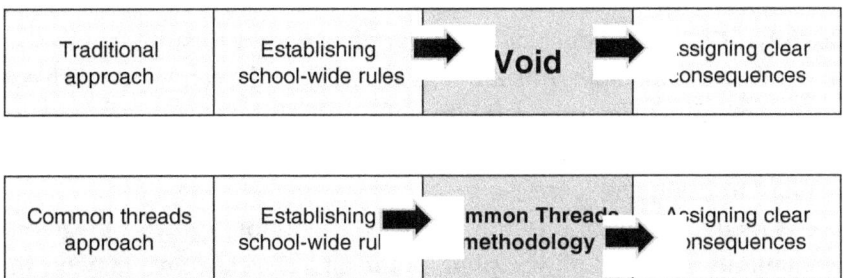

The Common Threads methodology provides for the gap by articulating process. In line with Marzano's findings, defining the nature of this step within the framework of discipline assists with establishing a safe environment, but also one that identifies and defines the code of behavior.

As we continue to witness legal decisions that turn fiction to fact, we must address our inconsistencies within our system to establish a more proactive, nonbiased mechanism to support our students and make us less susceptible to legal difficulties.

ISSUES OF CULTURE AND RACE

When it comes to a discipline structure, we would be remiss if we did not think about the effects of race and culture in our lives and in our schools. As with our family structures, the necessity to secure a positive initial relationship with our stakeholders is crucial; however, when we begin to consider the impact of race on these instances, we can start to see that trust building must be at the forefront of our mission.

Glenn Singleton and Curtis Linton, in *Courageous Conversations About Race*, discuss the impact of systematic racism and how it relates to schooling. Within his message, educators must join together in their understanding of issue like critical race theory to engage each other in conversations to bridge our understanding of cultures.[9] All voices in the process of creating trusting environments must be heard by facing the data with passion and resolve.

For instance, Martha Bireda, in *Eliminating Racial Profiling in School Discipline*, notes that discipline referrals are at an "all-time high for African American males."[10] As reports such as Bireda's start to tally, it is no wonder that many families do not trust the entities or the folks running them. It is the responsibility of the school to reach out to its community members (both white and of color) to join together in efforts to ensure equality for all. To do this, administrators must be willing to listen and learn.

As mentioned prior, discipline involves emotion. As we engage our community in issues of discipline, we must also realize we may be engaging our families of color in a negative fashion without even knowing it. Part of that issue can be adjusted by becoming educated when it comes to the systematic traits of our educational system, and part of the solution can be to utilize a consistent approach to investigating.

For example, there are many people that become extremely upset when they have to take their car for service. As educated people, we understand that machines do not last forever, and from time to time, they will break down and need to be repaired. However, folks tend to define the point of contention not around the car's imperfections but around not understanding the process (or details) associated with the repair and then receiving different price quotes from different service stations. Furthermore, trust wanes each time a person secures a new estimate from a different mechanic only to find the price and workload varies. These disparities contribute to the divide.

Staying with the topic of cars, how do you feel about used car salespeople? Although these people may be the most trustworthy, authentic people on the planet, the fact that their craft is undefined lends to the speculation that something is awry not with the system but with the person. In other words, without "seeing" a system to define the process, we are left with judging the person's actions as either ethical or not.

Marcus Simpson, in "The Impact of Schoolwide Positive Behavior Support on the Discipline Gap in the Middle School Setting," states that "African American students are overrepresented in school discipline referrals, creating what is known as the discipline gap. Research has shown that patterns in office disciplinary referrals can impact students' academic achievement."[11] The correlation to cars and students may seem absurd but can provide a glimpse of the complexity of the cultural issue.

Maybe some of our minority families see administrators as used car salespeople. Although our intentions may be genuine, the lack of consistency may breed disdain and mistrust. Perhaps the missing protocol presents our intentions in a similar light to a shyster trying to pawn a lemon to an unassuming customer. In a sense, by no fault of our own, we may be contributing to the "discipline gap" simply by not being able to vocalize our methodology and replicate it in a consistent fashion.

Tonya Sturgess, in her study "Does Discipline Only Skim the Surface? The Relationship between Teachers' Races and Student Discipline in Elementary and Secondary Schools," found that "both Black and White female teachers wrote significantly more referrals for Black male students than for White male students."[12] The disturbing nature of this study speaks to the predictability of the results. If the system is predictable, the solutions to fixing it must stem beyond the actions to our inherent belief systems that guide our actions.

Douglas McGregor, in *The Human Side of Enterprise*, created a hierarchy for understanding management's role in developing human beings. McGregor believed that individuals assumed one of two management styles.[13] First, theory X leaders did not see work as a joyous affair but one of disdain. These leaders felt that people were lazy by nature and, therefore, would need to be coerced into obtaining the end results. Conversely, theory Y leaders perceived work as a blissful experience, one leading to the greater good of the company mission and the individual. With this belief system, management's role would be to assist people in reaching their potential.

Perhaps the issue of culture and school discipline can be linked to some of McGregor's principles as they relate to the predictability of the discipline gap. Although it is not being suggested that administrators view minority students within the theory X framework, perhaps our minority families view administrators as such. Without a systematic approach to investigation, administrators might appear to be "lazy" when it comes to the task of defining disciplinary protocol. Without having the conversation or a trusting relationship prior to an incident, maybe our public views our efforts as duplicitous, which results in a disconcerting connection to one another.

Another way to view this concept is to consider conflict. Although, as school leaders, we recognize that conflicts do exist, oftentimes we have the ability to separate the action from the person by way of defining the process. For example, if two teachers were vying for a limited amount of funds for a special project, they might be more inclined to accept a decision knowing there was a protocol that was followed in determining the outcome rather than just an arbitrary decision made by the boss. Furthermore, by following a protocol, the relationship has the potential to sustain because the initial conflict was not solved by way of perceived impulse.

Culture also impacts those who are of the majority. All families need to know and understand that not only will the discipline code be followed but also the process leading up to the consequence and resolution was impartial. A healthy population promotes a healthy culture for all. The more voices in the conversation, the better chance we have at establishing what is right.

Securing a framework for investigations can assist administrators addressing situations with both white families and families of color by creating a common language that is based upon the action and not the person. In a sense, by capturing and replicating the investigative process, we can begin to educate our community and build the trust that is so desired in today's schools.

FOCUS ON SAFE SCHOOLS

Do you have a safe school? How do you know? Whose opinion matters more? Yours? The teachers? The parents? The students? How about the school board?

Much has been written concerning the heartbreaks of Columbine, Sandy Hook, and other school tragedies. Many schools have tried to adopt zero tolerance policies in an effort to make each school a safe place. However, with no formal system, how can we be certain that we are adhering to our goal of safety first?

Walk into any secondary school and ask if there is a systematic practice for investigations. Some will claim that there is a discipline code; others will state that they use Discipline with Dignity, Developmental Designs, or Restorative Practices. However, despite the usefulness and soundness of each (the code and different practices), none of these answers address the procedure for attaining facts.

School safety has much to do with school culture. Although no one can predict the uncanny, the actions and relationships between the people in the building lend themselves to the belief that the building is safe. Principals are at center stage in creating and securing a healthy, safe environment.

Wilma Bayko, in her study "Building Positive School Culture: The Principal's Journey," "concluded the tools for building culture that were key to the success experienced by the principals were the language they used and the relationships they built. The language in their communication with others needed to be inclusive, inviting, and supportive to ensure that people felt ownership of the culture."[14]

Language is often overlooked when it comes to building healthy relationships. The tasks of an administrator are exhausting. Days are marched at a blistering speed. Between student issues, parent issues, teacher issues, and such, today's administrator is in constant motion. However, despite the rapid pace, administrators must become introspective when it comes to the specific language we use when we are communicating to constituents.

Bayko's study concluded with several key recommendations. First, "Education programs [need to provide] opportunities for principals to examine their language patterns and belief systems as these are key in building relationships."[15] Further recommendations cited the need to assist principals by way of providing mentors for them. These concepts resonate, and the benefits of examining our linguistic patterns and being able to converse with an experienced administrator would certainly be sound advice.

Positive linguistic patterns provide the speaker and the one spoken to with a common starting place. Yet, in today's school offices, there does not seem to be a starting place for conversation when it comes to communicating the process of school discipline. Without a definable beginning, conversation between administrators and students and families suffer.

Too often, assumptions on the part of the administrators create a divide, even with the most genuine of people. For example, ask any administrator to review his or her discipline code and define what happens when a student makes a threat to a teacher. Certainly, even the most novice principal could open the code, turn to the page about threats, and then recite the consequences for said action. However, now ask the same administrator to define how he or she knew a threat was made. Here is where the gap exists.

Current discipline codes define negative actions (what a threat is) and also define the action's consequence (suspensions, expulsions, etc.), but the codes do not provide a rationale for how the initial action was founded. In not communicating to our constituents the critical component to the process, we create suspicion and assume trust for the discretionary component of the process.

Consider the research on school safety. Many learned texts have been produced discussing planning and preparation for school events. These texts, such as Kenneth Lane, Michael Richardson, and Dennis Van Berkum's *School Safety Handbook: Taking Action for Student and Staff Protection* or Michael Wanko's *Safe Schools: Crisis Prevention and Response*, provide safety plans and a host of other tactical resources to assist administrators in securing a safe environment.[16] What needs to accompany these valuable resources is the necessity to identify and define the traditionally undefined—the process of investigation, which is the hidden discretionary component by which much of these events originate.

Much of the focus on traditional relationship failures manifest in the topic of bullying. There are literally thousands of articles, books, and studies completed on the topic. At the root of most failures resides the imbalance of power on the part of the bully and the victim. Although commonplace analysis attempts to solve student-to-student conflicts, issues of power and control also exist in relations between adults and students, even when the adult bully is unaware of his or her actions.

The jury is still out on zero tolerance environments; however, the initial premise still remains. Zero tolerance calls for the health, welfare, and safety of our students to attain the most dynamic learning environment. Within this premise, discipline issues must be handled with the utmost resolve, maximizing the school's right to process consequences in order to attain feasible results. However, as stated prior, one of the most fundamental components to being able to even attempt a "zero tolerance" environment is the ability to sustain consistency within our investigative practice.

Sometimes there are instances when administrators need to levy serious consequences. For example, if the need should arise to place a student in an alternative setting, one should be able to define the specific protocol and facts prior to an expulsion hearing. Conversely, the inability to articulate said protocol could present an imbalance of power (a bullying situation).

Recall Walter Feinberg and Jonas Soltis with issues of fair and equal. When administrators fail to provide the specific documentation associated with a potential consequence, innuendoes of conspiracy germinate. The inability to explain compounds the investigation by drawing attention to our methodology rather than the incident at hand.

Furthermore, school boards want to feel confident that the correct consequence is being levied when making such a dramatic change of placement. During such hearings, administrators are called to testify by explaining the practice that one utilized in gathering the facts. Employing a systematic approach to these investigations could lend credibility to our position and confidence on behalf of school boards to make the tough decisions regarding alternative placements.

In addition, students are very intelligent individuals. They can recognize when an administrator has a system and follows through when it comes to handling discipline and referrals. Comments like "You can't fool her" are actually compliments for those who maintain consistency and equity within the discipline model. When students and parents know that issues will be addressed in a systematic, nonbiased manner, then confidence will gather momentum in attaining desired results not only on annual surveys but also and more importantly in the hallways and classrooms.

School cultures and configurations can drastically change the type of school safety planning that must be accomplished to ensure healthy environments. Likewise, the research available also confirms that when students feel safe (free from bullying), achievement is impacted.[17] Yet, repeatedly, educators are quick to look outside themselves for solutions to complex issues rather than using an introspective approach to our craft.

Could the lack of a formalize system be contributing to students (and adults) feeling unsafe? The answer to this questions lies within the confines of the personal school environment. Although the drastic garners the noteworthy news headlines, it is the day-to-day interactions between people that fashion and sustain the culture of the building. **Safe buildings start with safe relationships**. Being able to vocalize (to teach) a process breeds a deeper understanding and strengthens trusting relationships.

Traditionally, rank can and was applied to delineate power. Explanations that ended with "because I am the principal" used to work in an environment of dictated control. But just as administrators would cringe with a teacher's rationale to students to learn a certain skill because it was "on the test," so too should principals cultivate in themselves a greater standard of explanation.

True power comes not by way of rank but by learning and communicating. An administrator's work should encompass the need to continue to educate. Adopting and explaining a systematic approach to investigations will increase a principal's ability to sustain positive relationships and build trust when creating safer schools.

No one can predict the future. And unfortunately, no matter how hard we plan, there will inevitably be actions that occur in schools that are not well received. Perhaps a possible root cause to such tragedies starts with our inability to define and explain the systems that support school safety in the first place. By adopting a systems-based approach to investigation, we expose the void and can begin the critical conversations that can lead to trust and a more positive culture.

SYNOPSIS OF KEY CONNECTIONS

In closing, these five topics are some of the most prominent influences that are impacting education today. It is believed that these influences, along with the previously mentioned lack of consistency and common language for investigations, cause the current need to utilize a systematic approach to investigations.

The common threads model is a practical, systematic process that can be readily learned and adapted to any situation where an investigative methodology must take place. But prior to actually seeing how it works from a practical standpoint, it is critical to digest the research that supports such a method. When it comes to the backbone of solving school discipline, one need look no further than to the fundamentals of qualitative research.

NOTES

1. "The Rise and Effect of Single Parent Families," StudyMode, June 2008, www.studymode.com/.
2. Julia Richardson, "Avoidance as an Active Mode of Conflict Resolution," *Team Performance Management: An International Journal* 1, no. 4 (1995): 19–25.
3. Vanessa Elaine Domine, *Rethinking Technology in Schools* (New York: Peter Lang, 2009).
4. Allan G. Osborne and Charles J. Russo, *Discipline in Special Education* (Thousand Oaks, CA: Corwin, 2009).
5. Alberto M. Bursztyn, *Handbook of Special Education* (Lanham, MD: Rowman & Littlefield, 2008).
6. Antonis Katsiyannis and John W. Maag, "Manifestation Determination as a Golden Fleece," *Exceptional Children* 68, no. 1 (Fall 2001): 85–96.
7. Alexander W. Wiseman, *Principals under Pressure: The Growing Crisis* (Lanham, MD: Rowman & Littlefield, 2005).
8. Robert J. Marzano, *What Works in Schools* (Alexandria, VA: ASCD, 2003).
9. Glenn E. Singleton and Curtis Linton, *Courageous Conversations About Race: A Field Guide for Achieving Equity in Schools* (Thousand Oaks, CA: Corwin, 2006).
10. Martha R. Bireda, *Eliminating Racial Profiling in School Discipline: Cultures in Conflict* (Lanham, MD: Scarecrow, 2002).
11. Marcus Todd Simpson, "The Impact of Schoolwide Positive Behavior Support on the Discipline Gap in the Middle School Setting" (EdD diss., Walden Universtity 2010).

12. Tonya K. Sturgess, "Does Discipline Only Skim the Surface? The Relationship between Teachers' Races and Student Discipline in Elementary and Secondary Schools" (PhD diss., Capella University, 2011).

13. Douglas McGregor, *The Human Side of Enterprise* (New York: McGraw-Hill, 1960).

14. Wilma Alice Bayko, "Building Positive School Culture: The Principal's Journey" (PhD diss., University of Alberta, Canada, 2005).

15. Bayko, "Building Positive School Culture."

16. Kenneth E. Lane, Michael D. Richardson, and Dennis W. Van Berkum, eds., *The School Safety Handbook: Taking Action for Student and Staff Protection* (Lancaster, PA: Technomic Publishing, 1996); Michael Wanko, *Safe Schools: Crisis Prevention and Response*, Historical Dictionaries of Religions, Philosophies, and Movements (Lanham, MD: Scarecrow, 2001).

17. Joseph A. Dake, James H. Price, and Susan K. Telljohann, "The Nature and Extent of Bullying at School," *Journal of School Health* 73, no. 5 (May 2003): 173–80.

III

PRACTICAL APPLICATION

SETTING THE STAGE

A good friend of ours shared a story from his law school days. Routinely, he arrived at class ten minutes before the scheduled start time. He sat in his usual seat, put down his coffee in his usual spot, and reviewed notes from his readings and discussion points. As always, the ten minutes passed quickly. Without warning, an argument stumbled into the classroom and two men began to push each other, yelling and arguing. The heated argument quickly escalated into a full-blown fight, and desks were toppled. The class stared on in shock and disbelief.

Was this really happening at a revered Pennsylvania law school? What if the fight escalated into something more? What if one of them had a weapon? What started all of this? Could we be in danger? Some students stood up and backed away from the melee. Some shouted for the two people to stop. Others ran for help. As quickly as the fight began, it was over and the two perpetrators were out of the door and out of sight.

Stunned and bewildered, the class sat in awe of what just transpired right in front of them. Enter their professor. Calmly he walked to the board and wrote, "Write down everything that you just observed. Be specific. Stick to the facts." After about ten minutes of silent writing, the professor asked for volunteers to share their accounts.

One account spoke of two men, both with muscular build, one tall with dirty blonde hair and one on the short side with black hair. Students in the class shook their heads and murmured to each other.

"No way . . . they weren't muscular. One was slight in build. The other was average. And no one had dirty blonde hair. They both had black hair." Another student conceded that one could have had black hair, but the other had a skullcap on. Surely no one could tell what color hair the other had.

Another saw a knife in a carrying case on a belt. Another saw a cell phone case, not a knife case. One saw a punch thrown where others saw just hard shoving and pushing. The professor shook his head and smiled as the class rumbled with uncertainty and frustration. All of them "knew" what they had seen and heard. All of them had their definitive view of what happened. Or did they?

Of course, the fight was a setup. The professor had two upperclassmen stage an argument that happened to stumble into the classroom. Both men were dressed differently and had varying builds and physical features. No one had a knife, but one did have an iPod clip on his belt. The point had been made.

Where does truth lie when witnesses perceive varying accounts of any situation? Does personal bias start to play a role? Will people sensationalize an account to bolster a more dramatic story to capture a stronger reaction from the person who is listening so intently?

As individuals, it would be hard not to capture what we see and perceive in individualistic terms. We all remember what we want to remember. Our own life experiences, biases, prejudices, and attractions make each one of us more prone to honing in on what matters to us the most, or in some cases what scares us the most. How then can the truth really be discovered in any instance of uncertainty, especially when dealing with children in schools?

THE STEP-BY-STEP PROCESS

Disciplinary concerns exist in every school on every level. Finding the truth in investigations is a difficult task for school administrators and disciplinarians. the common threads model is a methodology that guides an investigation by isolating facts to draw educated conclusions. It is a sequential plan designed to remove subjectivity found in accusations that arise from investigations. The process relies on six steps described by the acronym THREAD.

Tap Your Resources
Handle Incident Reports
Review with an Interview
Examine the Chart
Address the Consequences
Decide on Future Planning

Incidents can occur at a school at any time. From these reports, our job as administrators is to engage in the process of investigating what happened in order to offer a resolution. Be it a student, teacher, parent, guidance counselor, or any other person that brings forth an issue they deem to need intervention, the process of common threads begins as soon as an initial report occurs. From the initial onset, the necessity to be organized and prepared to handle the investigation is vital to the success that one will attain. We begin the process by organizing our resources.

Step 1: Tap Your Resources

When starting the process of common threads, the facts have to be in the forefront. As stories unfold from the accounts of individuals, biases and perceptions can come into play. The entire process of common threads revolves around facts.

Organize Yourself

First, be sure to secure a place that you will be conducting the investigation. It may be your office, a guidance suite, or even a conference room. Just be sure that you have a place to conduct your work. In addition, be sure to have sufficient supplies for the investigations. Pens, clipboards, discipline books, and tissues should be mainstays for any investigation. Plus, be certain to supply yourself with several incident report (IR) sheets (see the scenarios for examples), as students will be utilizing these forms to document their accounts concerning the current incident.

Use Your People

Next, when investigating, bring in other professionals that have made connections with the students. Teachers, guidance counselors, other administrators, support staff members, and so forth, can be of tremendous assistance in any investigation. Using professionals that would not usually be seen delving for information creates a sense of security and safety for students and also broadens the perception of how important this investigation is for the people conducting it.

Arrange Your Witnesses

With any event, the investigator is looking to locate information. One of the best ways to secure such data is by chatting with people who were either involved in the incident or witnessed the event take place. As you begin to gather your witness list, be sure to plan your time accordingly so that each person can have a reasonable amount of time to complete the IR sheets. (Note: Even the students involved in the incident are at first considered part of the witness group to establish a level playing field for all.)

Step 2: Handle Incident Reports

Prior to the official interview, students will complete (in writing) an incident report sheet. IR sheets are guiding questions that focus the dialogue between the student and the investigator. From these questions, the investigator will be able to start to map out the events of the incident in order to attain what happened.

Welcome the Individuals

Upon the initial meeting, start by welcoming the student and ask how he or she is doing that day. Emphasize that this is a safe environment, and no other students know that he or she is here or what he or she is doing. Also reinforce that the student's anonymity will be protected throughout the process.

Complete the Incident Report Sheets

Once you have established a safe environment, simply hand the student an incident report sheet and ask the student to fill in the information to the best of his or her ability.

Do Not Offer the Witness Any Information

This will prevent the planting of any biased or influenced information that you as the investigator may already have. Say to them, "So something happened in the hall between second and third period today. Can you please tell me what you saw?" or "We're just following up on what happened in lunch today. Just write in your own words what happened." Nine times out of ten, students will shake their heads and start to write without further prompting.

If you get that puzzled "I don't have any idea what you are talking about" look, give another nugget of information that may joggle their memory. If they still don't respond, have them write that they have no knowledge of anything happening. The simple act of putting a denial in writing may joggle a few facts loose that otherwise a student may be unwilling to give because of being involved in the incident or not wanting to sell out friends.

Make Sure That the Student Fills Out the Entire Sheet

Remembering details such as witnesses, what time and date the incident happened, and where the incident occurred are great ways to joggle the memory. Perhaps trying to remember the most mundane details will enable a student to remember a point that may not have seemed important at the time but plays a vital part in piecing together an incident. Some of the most unimportant details of this process will revolve around who the student remembers may have also witnessed the incident.

Step 3: Review with an Interview

Once the individual completes his or her IR sheet, and you feel confident that the person has no more to write, it is time to review the text with the individual in the form of an interview. The interview is where these facts can begin to come into focus. Again, students must be interviewed individually and within certain guidelines so that the student is providing information, not being fed cues to come to conclusions that can be considered coerced in any way. If there are fifteen witnesses to an incident, there should be at least fifteen interviews if not more when other witnesses are discovered within those initial fifteen witnesses. Time consuming? Yes. However, this process will prove invaluable when completing a thorough and effective investigation.

Maintain a Secure Environment

The safer a student feels speaking to an investigator, the more willing he or she is going to be to give facts and possibly admit culpability in admitting their mistakes. After all, the purpose of discipline is ultimately to curb repeating negative behaviors and to have the student accept responsibility for being a productive citizen in our society. If that student feels safe to admit wrongdoing in front of you and accept consequences for his or her actions, the fact-finding missions in the future will be more productive and successful. You will start to realize what works and what does not work with your own style and strengths.

Review the IR Sheet

Take a moment and read the IR sheet in the presence of the individual who wrote it. In understanding, we are not looking to have a perfect grammatical essay, only a legible version describing the events of the incident. If you do not understand what was written, ask the individual for clarification. These types of checks assist with building an understanding and also help with the validity of what is being presented. Remember, you are only looking for information that the student saw firsthand; you do not want hearsay. (Note: If a student needs assistance [e.g., special education needs, 504 needs, etc.], be sure to secure it prior to chatting with the student.)

Look for Action Statements

Take each IR sheet and start to look for actions that occurred within the testimony of the witness. For example, if someone states that a person "hit" someone, that action would be charted into a box (step 4). Again, when questioning the witness, try to elicit as many specific descriptions as possible. Asking for clarification or even demonstration can help to define a "hit" from a "slap." In many cases, the more specific the information, the more genuine the connection and easier it will be to prove.

Realize Someone Could Be Withholding Truth

How does anyone ever know what is truth and what is not true when dealing with kids of any age, especially when "getting in trouble" may be on the agenda? Knowing this point, when interviewing children, always remind them to please stay on topic and stay focused on exactly what they saw, heard, touched, tasted, and smelled.

In addition to collecting only the facts, pay attention to when you think a child is not being honest with you. Watch their eyes. Check for fidgeting limbs, watch their breathing, and talk to them about it. Let the student know that he or she is displaying some traits of a person that looks uncomfortable. Allow the student to respond without saying much of anything. Silence is usually all it will take to garner what really happened. We are not attempting to claim expertise in psychology; however, noting changes in a student's behavior may just lead to a break in the dialogue.

Thank and Assure the Witness

In maintaining a professional approach, it is always a great idea to thank each individual witness and assure him or her that this testimony will remain anonymous. In realizing that investigations are not static, you may have to chat with this person later, especially if that person was either a victim or participant in the actual event. Be sure to mention that you may need to speak further to them about the situation.

The Role of the Police in the Investigation Process

From time to time, students will commit crimes in school. These crimes could range from theft, to bullying and offenses involving drugs and alcohol. The common threads process can be useful in helping the appropriate law enforcement agencies to gather facts and decide what consequences, if any, need to be issued to offending students. However, principals need to follow all specific district protocols. Since the involvement of law enforcement in disciplinary situations varies from district to district, refer to policy and central office administration for guidelines, policy, and steps to ensure appropriate actions.

The Role of the Media in the Investigation Process

Just as law enforcement may become involved in some incidents, the media may also be an entity that school administrators must deal with, especially when a hot topic like bullying or substance abuse is concerned. Follow all guidelines, policies, and protocols to handle members of the press. Never try to handle the press on your own, as this could lead to miscommunication or misquoting, which could potentially damage the progress of an investigation. Remember that the press wants a story that will attract readers or viewers. They could sensationalize an incident to make it more attractive for the public, which could ultimately portray your best intentions in a negative light.

Step 4: Examine the Chart

Once all of the witnesses have completed their IR sheets and have had their interview, it becomes time to analyze the chart and start to build connections. These connections, much like the qualitative conceptual framework, will begin to yield the reality of the insiders' (witnesses') perspective.

Chart the Data

It is now time to chart your action statements. From our incident reports, the administrator takes a few moments to complete the chart by placing the action statements in the most logical order of events (most time that order is chronological). Once all IR sheets have been charted, one can begin to develop a clearer picture of what occurred.

Find the Threads

Table 3.1 shows an example of three witnesses that provided what they saw, heard, and felt during an incident. The facts that they provided are both common and varied in nature. There are consistencies and inconsistencies. The investigator's job at this point in the process will be to identify common denominators. Highlight the common details, and discount outliers (or claims that are not substantiated through common observations).

As table 3.2 illustrates, the investigator now has a focused idea of what transpired during the incident. From the highlighted areas, the investigator can deduce the following: (1) Rita hit Trudy; (2) Trudy tripped Rita; and, finally, (3) both Rita and Trudy threatened each other. In addition, the investigator can infer that the evidence does not support Rita's claim that Trudy cursed during the incident.

Joan	Rita	Trudy	Ed
Saw Rita hit Trudy	Says Trudy hit her	Says Rita hit her	Saw Rita hit Trudy
Saw Trudy trip Rita	Trudy tripped her	Accidently tripped Rita	Didn't see a trip
Didn't hear cursing	Trudy cursed	Didn't hear cursing	Didn't hear cursing
Said Rita threatened Trudy in the hall after lunch	Says she threatened Trudy in response to her threat	Says she threatened Rita in response to her threat that Rita issued first	Didn't hear a threat

	Joan	Rita	Trudy	Ed
	Saw Rita hit Trudy	Says Trudy hit her	Says Rita hit her	Saw Rita hit Trudy
	Saw Trudy trip Rita	Trudy tripped her	Accidently tripped Rita	Didn't see a trip
	Didn't hear cursing	~~Trudy cursed~~	Didn't hear cursing	Didn't hear cursing
	Said Rita threatened Trudy in the hall after lunch	Says she threatened Trudy in response to her threat	Says she threatened Rita in response to her threat that Rita issued first	Didn't hear a threat

	Joan	Rita	Trudy	Ed	Mr. G. (Adult)
	Saw Rita hit Trudy	Says Trudy hit her	Says Rita hit her	Saw Rita hit Trudy	Saw Rita hit Trudy
	Saw Trudy trip Rita	Trudy tripped her	Accidently tripped Rita	Didn't see a trip	Trudy tripped Rita
	Didn't hear cursing	Trudy cursed	Didn't hear cursing	Didn't hear cursing	No cursing
	Said Rita threatened Trudy in the hall after lunch	Says she threatened Trudy in response to her threat	Says she threatened Rita in response to her threat that Rita issued first	Didn't hear a threat	Heard Rita threaten Trudy only

Oftentimes at this juncture of the process, we are asked about the credibility of an adult witness. When dealing with a teacher (or another adult) as a witness, certain considerations need to be taken into account when reviewing their re-creation of the events. Table 3.3 shows the inclusion of an adult that witnessed the event into the mix of the investigation.

With the addition of a professional into the investigation, emphasis is placed upon his or her account. This does not mean that what the adult witness says is set in stone. However, since this is an adult or a colleague with no perceivable competing interest in student politics, the adult's word must be taken at a more intense level. We wish that there was a magic formula or equation that provided how much "weight" should be computed to make that sort of determination, but every case has its individual players and circumstances.

As a rule, teachers and other adults have been through many situations in their lives that entitle them to a higher status when reporting facts. Their wisdom and observation skills are more acute and, therefore, more reliable. However, if an adult is a witness and has procured a tendency to exaggerate or treat students with a bit of unfairness in the past, your judgment as the investigator can weigh into the validity of the adult's observations.

Luckily, in this case, Mr. G. verifies much of what the investigator knows. However, the fact that Mr. G. heard Rita threaten Trudy solidifies the evidence that Rita was involved in a threat. The validity of the claim that Trudy had made a threat is not in question, as Trudy admitted to making a threat toward Rita in her interview. (Note: Even if Trudy had not admitted to the threat, a conversation can usually draw this information out of a student with the facts that are already present.)

Another point to remember when going through this process is to rely on the facts and only the facts. Being as specific as possible diminishes the opportunities to explain the facts instead of reporting them. For example, Trudy explained that she "accidentally" tripped Rita. As the investigator, comments such as "I accidentally did it" or "I was just messing around; I was never serious" cannot come into play. The facts must be presented to the students as they happened. Trudy tripped Rita. Rita hit Trudy. Both girls threatened each other (regardless of who threatened whom first). The facts remain that each of these details happened, and details are what determine consequences.

Step 5: Address the Consequences

At the conclusion of step 4, it is time to inform the student of the facts that were found in the investigation. Students will be nervous, scared, and at times, belligerent during this process. Students are thinking about nothing more than "what will my consequence be? Am I going to be suspended? What will my parents say?" Students are human beings. They are dealing with heightened emotions and are facing dire consequences in the realities of what their lives revolve around. Always keep this in mind when speaking to students.

Present the Facts

In this step, the administrator would present the results of the common threads to the students. Be sure to go through the entire process. In addition, do not review the facts in a group. If four students are involved, have four meetings. This is paramount in obtaining honest reactions and possible confessions. Start from the beginning and move through each step and each fact until you reach the conclusions. Upon hearing the evidence, it is at this point that most students will admit to their specific roles in the incident. If the students still deny their role in the event, you have the evidence to proceed in making an educated and fact-based conclusion.

Never Raise Your Voice

Once an investigator raises his or her voice, it puts that student on the defensive and the opportunity for discussion is lost. Stay calm and in control of the situation. The investigator must take the lead when meeting with a student. No matter how frustrated or angry an investigator may be, he or she can leave the situation to take a breather. When a situation presents itself, and you feel that you are about to raise your voice, be sure to take a walk, get a glass of water, or simply take a deep breath outside of the room, but never, ever lose your cool in front of a student.

If Need Be, Show the Chart

In some cases, you may feel it necessary to show the chart. In addition to explaining the facts, present the grid and articulate the conclusions that are being made through evidence. This will be extremely beneficial for visual learners and will also show a student just how much evidence has been collected through the process. Be sure not to identify any witnesses on the grid. Remove all traces of personal identity. Do not use initials. Use "student A" or "number 1" as your identifiers.

Explain the Importance of Honesty and Integrity

After defining and showing the process, explaining how important it is to be honest will work in helping the student learn from the incident and impacting the student's actions the next time he or she is presented with a similar circumstance. It will also establish a connection and bond between the two of you when you are ready to assign the consequence for that student's actions. In soliciting an honest response, there are a couple of quick techniques that may assist you in the process.

First, have a small mirror in your office. Set it up on the end of your desk facing outward. Have the following statement printed on it: "Always be proud of the person you see in front of you." Make sure that the mirror is in sight of students as you are speaking to them. In this fashion, perhaps a student will realize that you cannot fool the person in the mirror.

Another great tip is to talk about "the second mistake." Explain that everyone makes mistakes. The important thing is to learn from each mistake. Participating in the incident was the first mistake. Encourage students to not make the second mistake by not taking responsibility for the first.

Explain the Implications and Consequences of the Student's Actions

As the investigator explains the consequences outlined in the discipline code, make sure to include that it is the actions of the student that has earned the student this consequence and that he or she violated the discipline code. This way, the implementation of discipline becomes less personal. The student's actions incurred the discipline, not the personalization of an administrator that is "out to get" them.

What the Other Students "Got" Is of No Concern

One of the first questions any investigator will get from a student will be, "Well, what did the other kid get?" Luckily, the quick answer is, "I cannot tell you that information. It is against the law. The Family Educational Rights and Privacy Act, FERPA, prohibits me from doing so, but I can assure you that I have followed the discipline code to the fullest extent."

Never Call Anyone a Liar

Kids will at times not tell the truth, or will conveniently leave important bits or evidence out of a factual account. Instead of getting angry or upset (especially when you have the evidence that supports the truth), talk to them. Have the conversations that will lead to their heart and conscience. Explain that everyone makes mistakes and bad choices, and they will recover from this situation. Most of the time, a student will come around and tearfully admit their culpability. And if not, you have the evidence to support the decision of finding them guilty after the investigation. Just because a student does not admit to something does not mean he or she did not commit the act.

Call Parents in the Presence of the Student

Call Mom, Dad, or the student's guardian while the student is with you in the office. Explain the situation to the family member or allow the student to do so. In this fashion, the family member will receive one version of the story at the same time from both you and the child. In addition, when communicating to the family member, focus on the student's actions. Stay positive. (Communicating with family members is expanded upon in the section titled "Conversations with Parents and Guardians.")

Withhold Judgment

Human nature dictates certain results upon completing an investigation of any kind. One of these results is judgment. Although we all have personal codes of morality, the urge to judge must be oppressed. When dealing with students, passing judgment on an individual comes with bias and personalization. That's when investigators can get themselves into trouble. If situations or individuals are personalized, subjectivity can impact a fair and unbiased investigation, blurring results and casting doubt over the investigator's methods and reliability for this incident and the next one as well. Your decisions are going to be put under scrutiny no matter what conclusions are made with any amount of evidence, even if the evidence is indisputable. Why place yourself in a position where you may have to justify personal feelings that are not supported by data?

Rely on the Facts

Let the evidence support the reasoning. If your district has a discipline code, follow it. This way, it becomes less about the investigator and more about following a preestablished set of principles that the student chose to violate. It takes the personalization and opinions out of the mix . . . and clears your culpability for blame in the matter.

Step 6: Decide On Future Planning

After you establish what occurred and have administered the appropriate consequence for the action, it becomes time to consider a future course of action. However, you must realize that this important step can only come into consideration after every determination has been made through facts leading to culpability and after receiving a consequence (if there is one).

Establish the Why

During discipline situations, teaching lessons becomes an almost improbable task due to the mental state of the individuals involved. These times call for calmer situations and, thus, cannot be compromised in emotional moments. In this sense, establishing the "why" of an event before completing the entire investigative process could be detrimental to the integrity of the actual investigation and could lead to bias, judgment, and a questionable outcome.

In most investigations, students will provide reasons for why they punched their classmate or decided to vandalize their neighbor's locker. Listen to the reasons. Sympathize. Offer suggestions for help (counseling, restitution, and apologizing) and hand down their consequence with dignity and respect. When an administrator is thorough and consistent, the consequence will not be taken as a personal act of vengeance. It will be an outlined consequence that has been previously addressed in a discipline code or other form of documentation. It will not be personal. It will be a practical consequence for a bad decision.

The "why" behind the event can give us insight into the motivation behind the action and assist us in planning for the future, but it cannot excuse the action. Only in extreme situations is it recommended that the facts of an infraction be dismissed due to the circumstances of the event.

Use Proactive Guidance

Your guidance counselor will be your first line of assistance in disciplinary situations. Guidance counselors are trained to understand and interpret the inner workings of our kids. They have foresight into family issues, behaviors, and tendencies that will help you speak to children and form bonds with them that may not be possible without their help. After an incident, make sure that your guidance team understands exactly what has happened and involve them in proactive counseling or programs that will deal with the issues that created the incident in the first place. Do not, however, involve the counseling team in the actual disciplining of a student. It will compromise the integrity of the counselor's trust and will lead to future issues with the student–guidance counselor dynamic.

Use Positive Discipline Programs

Restorative Practices and programs like it work. Getting students together to discuss what impact their decisions have on other people forms connections. Letting a student know exactly how much anguish or inconvenience he or she has caused another person can be highly effective, especially when the victim can voice those feelings in a safe and neutral setting. Use these programs, and be proactive to hopefully avoid disciplinary situations in the first place. Just make sure if a situation does happen, you process the investigation first, without prejudice or bias.

Employ Peer-to-Peer Interaction

After the incident has concluded and consequences issued, it is important to have the involved students come together to make sure that the issue is over and all parties have moved on. Students that have not let situations go must be dealt with through counseling or other forms of communication. Retaliation is always a concern of children, especially after facts have been proven through the testimony of another. The consequences for any sort of retaliation must be clearly stated before the incident is put to bed. Peer-to-peer interaction is a necessary and fulfilling aspect of placing closure on any situation. It allows for both parties to voice final thoughts before moving on with life in school and can be a great release for the anxiety that can remain after a tough situation.

Utilize Outside Agencies When Necessary

Calling in the support of outside agencies may be warranted in cases of suspected abuse or if children present themselves as a danger to themselves or others. If abuse of any kind is suspected, the investigator must contact that agency immediately, no matter what stage the investigation is in. Following the law supersedes any need to complete a school investigation.

WHAT-IF SCENARIOS

Of course, investigations of this nature are not always as clean and easy as the Trudy and Rita incident. The only constant variable in the common threads process is that there are no constant variables. Each investigation will introduce the investigators to new and unforeseen complications and discoveries. This unpredictability is what makes this process human and interesting. Like everything that happens with people, nothing is conventional, and the journey of discovery will take investigations to different planes with various outcomes.

The simple basis of this process still remains its stronghold. If investigators can stay with the facts and assign consequences for those specifics, the process is a success. Below are common what-ifs that will complicate and compound investigations. Although potentially problematic, each situation can be solved by using sound reasoning and judgment.

What If There Are No Witnesses?

At times, a situation will present itself where there are no witnesses to an incident. In this case, truth may reside on one person's word against the other. But which person is telling the truth? Which person is detailing the most accurate account of what happened? First be sure to follow the process. Have each student write his or her account using an IR sheet. In this manner, the investigator is assured that this person will have to give his or her account twice (once in writing and once in the interview process).

Next, when involved in the interview, do not show the person the IR sheet. Ask the person to give the account from memory. Listen to exactly what each student is saying. Take your notes, and allow yourself some time to think about each scene as it is described by each person. If you happen to uncover inaccuracies in one person's account (from the IR sheet to the interview), it may be enough to decide on someone's behalf. In addition, once a lie is detected, everything that is said by that person would certainly have to be questioned.

Likewise, you may have situations where you are truly stumped on what happened and where truth lies. Although your instinct may tell you that truth is somewhere in the middle, without clear facts (or at least a clear direction of where the facts reside), it is not recommended that one assigns consequences based upon this simple maxim. In other words, be as sure as possible when administering each consequence.

What If Witnesses Are Using Past Incidents as Current Evidence?

One of the most common mistakes that investigators make in searching for answers in an incident is using past instances to draw conclusions about current situations. No matter what has happened in the past, those details cannot interfere with the investigation at hand. An investigator may also find that some witness testimony may have relevance for an incident that led up to the current situation. For example, one student may report that "another student hit my friend and called him names." You may inquire, "When did this happen?" If the answer is, "Well . . . it was about two months ago," we must remove these details from the current incident. The investigator may open another investigation for what happened two months ago, but he or she should not merge the situations together. This practice can lead to a skewed conclusion because of mounting evidence and inaccurate fact reporting.

In addition, in numerous cases, the student may have already received consequences for those actions if an investigation was concluded. Let the discipline code determine consequences for repeat offenses, not the investigation into individual scenarios.

What If an Adult (Who Did Not See the Event) Is Making the Accusation?

This situation can be tricky to navigate. Teachers, along with other professionals in the building, expect to be heard and can oftentimes insist on action when making accusations against a student's indiscretion. However, it is not the job of the investigator to accept anyone's word as "the truth" without a fair and impartial process of disseminating the facts.

Obviously, teachers and other adults' words must be considered at a heightened level. They are adults. They have the life experience and wisdom of what is fair and just. However, when an adult presents information that is not substantiated (guessing, assumptions, bias, etc.), the investigator needs to explain to that professional that facts are what create common threads, not hearsay or opinion.

We find that communication is paramount when investigating any incident. Reaching an unpopular decision may take some creative communication, including team meetings and faculty meetings to explain the process without violating anyone's rights or privacy. One may have to inform an adult that there is nothing that can be done immediately concerning a current situation. It is better to have a dialogue about the process and experience that potential uncomfortable moment than allow the unexplained results to fester into other arenas.

What If You Believe There Is a Witch Hunt?

When a student develops (or in some cases arrives with) a past reputation for breaking the rules, the radar is going to be on alert for anything that this child does. Unfair? Yes, but this situation can be a reality. If Billy is known to bully smaller students in the bathrooms, teachers may be reluctant to hand Billy a bathroom pass. In addition, teachers (and investigators) may be quick to point a finger at Billy if anything negative happens in a bathroom.

When investigating, be impartial. If Billy's name arises as a possible "contributor" to an incident, investigate where he was and what he was doing at the time of the incident. If facts prove he may have been part of it, continue. If not, move on and clear his name. Again, move on and clear his name. It is our responsibility to fight against this branding practice. And when facts pave the way, even the most severe of witch hunts will be branded inconclusive.

What If the Incident Occurred Three Weeks Ago?

Is there a statute of limitations on investigations? No. When you have those rare cases where incidents go unresolved, never close them down. Evidence may surface weeks and even months from the actual time line of events. Just make sure to keep incidents separate and never combine information to support the previous incident.

For example, if an investigator finds a piece of stolen property that went missing months ago while he or she was searching for an unrelated piece of stolen property in the present, process both pieces as separate incidents. Just because the previous piece was not located at the time the investigation happened does not mean the student should not be held accountable for those actions without a fair investigation.

What If I Get a Confession? Do I Still Need to Follow the Process?

Any investigation is made easier by obtaining a confession. When other parents or guardians question a disciplinary decision, the statement "He confessed to the accusation" can prove to be beneficial. However, despite obtaining the confession, be sure to still go through the process. The reason it is so critical to continue the process is due to the fact that people can and often do change their stories. What once seemed a "slam dunk" may put the investigator into a tailspin if the investigator does not have the facts to support the decision. Even though the confession assists an investigator in determining what happened, utilize the process as if a confession never occurred. In this manner, one will be able to feel secure that no matter what variations occur, the justification for the outcome will not have to be changed.

What If Someone Threatens to Go to Your Boss?

One of the realities of being in a position that deals with the public is that sooner or later, someone will ultimately not agree with your decision and wish to take it "to the next level." The key to this situation is not to take this person's decision as a personal affront. One of the best ways of securing such a balanced response is to stay to the system. Parents and guardians care about their children. If they truly feel that a mistake was made in dealing with their child, it is their right as taxpayers to be able to sit down and discuss the outcome with your immediate supervisor. When informed of their decision, remain professional and cordial. Once they leave your office, be sure to contact your supervisor and let him or her know of the person's decision. Share your protocol with your supervisor and be confident in the data.

CONVERSATIONS WITH PARENTS AND GUARDIANS

Speaking with parents and guardians of the students who are being disciplined is without a doubt one of the most demanding aspects of the discipline process. These folks are responsible for their children, and oftentimes, can take their child's disciplinary issues personally. However, there may be specific reasons behind a parent's actions.

Perhaps the "uncooperative parent" is that child's only advocate in life. Protecting their child's reputation and innocence is not only their responsibility but also their mission.

It is our charge to become that parent's partner in creating a safe environment to handle their child's indiscretions. With a parent on our side, success becomes more eminent for everyone. Plus, even if the parent is ultimately not on our side, we are going to need to make our case so clear that the facts speak for themselves. Here are a few suggestions to communicate with family members during discipline situations:

Start with a Greeting

Getting a call from your child's school is never without anxiety. Too often, it usually means something is wrong. Your child might be sick, hurt, not doing well academically, or in some sort of trouble. Start every greeting by saying that the child is fine. "Good morning, Mr. Jones. This is Sam Thomas from Sally's school. *Sally is fine. She's safe and sound right in front of me* . . ." You will literally feel the anxiety level of the parent decrease over the phone. In addition, you become more human. If you show the parents that you have enough concern for their role as parents (and what really matters—their child's safety), the parent will find it more difficult to become defensive when you are explaining the facts of the situation.

Speak Slowly and Sincerely

After your initial greeting, state, "Your child was involved in an incident at school, and if you have a few minutes, I would like to discuss it now." Oftentimes, we need to call people while they are at work. Do not assume that the parent can speak right this minute. Give them the option. This will build trust and lessen the initial anxiety. Next, be sure to have the evidence in front of you. Do not waste your time or theirs. Speak directly and explain the situation and the process you utilized to obtain the facts. You are merely reporting facts that coincide with consequences that have been previously outlined in a school code.

If Need Be, Ask for a Face-to-Face Meeting

Sometimes, a phone call may not suffice when it comes to more complex situations. In those instances, it might be better to request a meeting. When it comes to the dialogue between you and the family, again remember to be professional and genuine. Stay calm, speak slowly, and check for understanding. If need be, show the chart to the family and detail your protocol so that they understand you "took your time" with this incident. This will show that you cared about the outcome just as much as they do.

Remember the Positives

Just because a person has made a mistake does not diminish those redeeming qualities that we all possess. Try to accent those traits as they present themselves throughout the process. For example, if a student told the truth in the investigation, be sure to acknowledge and celebrate that point with the parent. This sharing may not be praise to you in handling the situation but may ease the tension by acknowledging the positive.

Show the Process

When communicating to the parents in person or by phone, communicate the process that you went through to reach your conclusions. It is important that families realize the impact that their child had on the school and the thoroughness that you go through to get the facts. We all want our children to be treated fairly and with respect. If you leave room for a parent to find a weakness in your process, they may be more apt to challenge everything that you have prepared.

If need be, rehearse the process before the meeting or phone call with a counselor or another administrator. Role-play. You may just catch a bit of shaky evidence or a question that you had not thought of before. Just remember that you can never use another child's name when reporting to a parent. That would be a violation of federal law that protects children's rights in school (FERPA).

Remember FERPA

The Family Educational Rights and Privacy Act of 1971 protects all students from violations of privacy coming from public school personnel. Only staff members with a vested interest in a student's educational well-being can relate personal information. This means that when a parent says, "What is the name of this other student that you keep referring to who helped start this food fight?" you can only respond by saying, "I cannot share that information; however, you can feel free to talk to your daughter about that."

If they ask what discipline the other student is getting, you again can only respond that the other student is being dealt with according to the discipline code, but you cannot share any other information as it is against the law. Although there are instances where student information must be shared (safety, threats, etc.), the safest bet is to follow the law.

Remember It Is Never Personal

All administrators will reach a point in their careers where a parent will be angry about a decision made about their child. Always maintain your composure (I know, easier said than done), and remind parents that this process is never personal. Rules are put into place to maintain a high standard of accountability so that an entire society has the opportunity to receive an education in a safe and nonthreatening environment.

If a child breaks those rules, there has to be consequences. These consequences will hopefully discourage a student from repeating negative or unacceptable behavior according to the discipline code. If you treat a child with dignity, follow the code and investigate with confidence that your methods have reached a conclusion to the best of your ability, and then feel confident in your decisions even when parents contradict those beliefs.

Do Not Endure an Abusive Situation

If a parent is being abusive or threatening in a manner that makes you feel insecure for your health, welfare, and safety, it is okay to end the conversation or meeting. Politely announce that the meeting is over and kindly escort the parent to the door. If you are on the phone, politely announce that you will not accept being yelled at and the conversation is over. If the parent keeps yelling, quietly hang up the phone. Again, stay calm. Your professionalism will be commended if and when the situation continues on a higher level. Be sure to contact your supervisor and let him or her know of the events so that there are no surprises or misunderstandings.

HELPFUL TIPS IN HANDLING FREQUENT SCENARIOS

As stated prior, every investigation is different. Whether one is dealing with diverse people, places, or circumstances, each investigation brings interesting and new challenges for an administrator. However, in realizing that these differences exist, there are also times when situations that present themselves seem eerily familiar. Déjà vu? Perhaps, but we like to associate these commonalities as patterns that students will sometimes utilize in their reasoning. By recognizing these patterns, and utilizing these helpful suggestions, one will be able to handle each instance with confidence.

The "I Didn't Do Anything" Declaration

When a child sits across from you, sometimes in tears, and is pleading that he or she "didn't do anything" and that all of the witnesses "are lying," it may become difficult to see the truth. Is this possible that a group of schoolchildren would go to such lengths as to get another student in this much trouble? It is possible but not likely. From our experience, school-age children do not have the wherewithal, time, or perseverance to create a web of lies that would extend to that level or attention spans to create that elaborate system "just to get someone."

Even though we cannot guarantee that this situation could occur, our best bet is to stay with the facts. Ask the accused student if he or she knows anyone else who saw the incident but is not involved with this certain group of friends or someone who does not readily know the student, that is, someone objective. Following the system and trusting your investigation is the greatest asset we have in this situation.

The "I Won't Snitch" Mentality

A surprisingly large movement in youth culture, the "I won't snitch mentality," has broadened and reached every student in our schools. This warped code of ethics can make the investigative process much more difficult when trying to identify names and accomplices in any incident. Children will protect the identities and actions of other children they do not even necessarily respect, like, or endorse just to protect their own identity of not being a "snitch." The most important thing an investigator can do right at the start of an interview is establish that everything said in your presence will be considered confidential and that the student's name will not be revealed. You, as the investigator, must always protect the identities of the students you decide to interview and think through the possible consequences of keeping your sources confidential and safe from revealing their identities. Investigators will find that most children will want to give you as much information as possible; children know their world will be safer if there are consequences for children that break the rules and if these children receive some justice.

The only assurance he or she needs is to be safe from being known as the one who gave up the information and how he or she will be perceived in the general public if identified as a "snitch." With a little careful questioning and planning, an effective investigation will be able to protect all sources and come out with the facts needed to proceed.

The "I Don't Know Anything" Stance

When questioning someone who is presumably guilty and is continuing to deny his involvement, ask for witnesses that can corroborate their story. Most likely the student will rattle off two or three of his or her best friends that will agree with his or her story without much prodding. Gladly take the names and call some of those students to be interviewed. When fact finding, the more information is found, the better the result will be. Before dismissing that student from interviewing, say, "In addition to these three people, can you give me the name of one or two people that were there that are not your friends? It will really help round out my investigation if I can get some information from some people that do not know you." Even if that student cannot or refuses to provide anyone else, the seed is planted that you are not finished checking into this event.

The "It Doesn't Matter, You Won't Believe Me Anyway" Defense

Quite simply, it does not matter how many times you see a student. Treat every incident as a brand new offense. Some students will sit across from you as an investigator and honestly believe that no matter what they say, you will find them guilty. This can be a defense mechanism or simply a diversion tactic to guilt you into not seeing the facts clearly.

Never prejudge; never assume that the child has done anything wrong "just because he or she is sitting across from you again"; and always stay focused on the facts of the incident. Repeat offenders will more likely be judged without facts by people who are not directly involved (certain staff members, other students, parents, etc.). However, as an investigator, you have the charge and responsibility to see the child sitting across from you as a brand-new case with brand-new facts. Use cumulative offenses as the discipline code may state, but never condemn a student's involvement in an incident without the proper investigative techniques outlined in this process.

The "This Is So Unfair" Argument

There will be times when students receive different disciplines for committing the same offense. It is always the investigator's responsibility to communicate this fact to parents and involved staff before too much time passes and rumors of favoritism or biased decision making begin to circulate. Of course, these reactions of being "unfair" will always be present in some form or another, but with some good "public relations" from the investigator, much of the negative impact can be set off. Explaining that every child is different and that each offense is evaluated separately can go far. Even stating that a student's history of disciplinary actions is not discussed can help.

The truth is, the investigation is no one else's business except for the administration, the student, and that student's family to what consequence he or she receives. FERPA reinforces this and is a guaranteed conversation ender to any complaint issued by a third party weighing in on what he or she feels is true justice. You are the investigator. You make the disciplinary calls. It is easy to be a Monday-morning quarterback, even in disciplinary incidents in a school setting. Make your informed decision, share it with the relevant parties, and move forward with confidence.

LIMITATIONS OF COMMON THREADS

How do you know that you have reached the truth in an investigation? It is a question that will plague you from time to time. The honest answer is "you do not." What you have done is followed a system of investigation and deduction that leads to facts to reconstruct a certain thread of events that constitutes a theory of happenings. These happenings lead to a hypothesis of what actually happened in an incident. Confessions clear up most of the ambiguity of a complicated matter, but you will not always get the confession. You are then charged with making an informed determination of the incident and come to a conclusion that will impact students and their families.

As with any solid qualitative analysis, limitations to the research must be presented in order to identify possible problems. Processes are not perfect; therefore, the necessity to expose the known deficiencies will ultimately provide a more robust conclusion. In this section, we offer some topics that we have heard and some topics that we face on a day-to-day basis.

There Is No Way to Find the Truth Every Time

Exactly. As the old saying goes, there are three versions of the truth in an investigation: your version, my version, and the truth, which is always somewhere in the middle. The ultimate goal of this system is not necessarily to find the concrete truth. It is to find facts that can construct a semblance of what has happened so the "truth" can present itself. Stick with the facts. They are impossible to argue. In addition, even though the old adage of "truth is found somewhere in the middle" may be utilized in schools, it does not account for each occurrence. Truth may reside in one person's story. It may be in the middle. It may be in neither. However, by following the system, you will have a better chance to find it.

Detractors of the Process Will Fight It

There will always be outliers that will fight against any system. The key is not to fight the detractors. Agree with them. Then present the indisputable facts that surround their arguments. Opinions and conjecture will always lead to criticism. Facts are concrete and will stand against any sort of argument. Use them to your advantage.

The Process Takes Time

In understanding that the tasks of school officials never cease, adding "one more thing" to an already overburdened audience may be met with contempt. There is no denying that the process does take time to accomplish but no more so than investigators have already allotted to locating facts. Plus, "a stitch in time saves nine." Better to spend a few extra moments on the proactive side than to spend countless hours defending our personal protocols.

"We Already Have a Discipline Code"

In understanding that many school districts already have their own discipline codes for deciphering consequences, we must separate this process from the code. Common threads makes using the code more concise by streamlining the investigative process. Discipline codes are designed to react to actions. The common threads process should be utilized prior to ever glancing at the code.

"You Did Not Ask the Individual to Explain Why the Action Occurred on the IR Sheet"

Understanding why an incident took place is truly valuable to interpreting motive and coming to a better place to plan for the future of all involved. However, we must always establish what occurred first. Leading with opinions on circumstance would only interfere with the investigation at this junction of the process. We secure plausible "whys" after we have established (to the best of our ability) what happened.

BENEFITS OF COMMON THREADS

Our ultimate goal in our schools today is to create an environment where students can reach their potential as learners and as human beings. With this belief statement, our decisions must be anchored to topics that give each student the best possibility to succeed. As we have explored the need for a systematic approach to investigations in schools, we have mentioned various benefits concerning the use of the common threads process. The following outlined factors are considered to be the top benefits to applying this system.

Consistency

The consistent approach of common threads is its hallmark. Processing discipline will never make anyone popular. The common threads systematic approach to fact finding will make the process judgment free and efficient. It is difficult to dispute facts and evidence when they are laying in front of a student in an organized, nonconfrontational system.

Common Language

By utilizing a specific and defined process, investigators in the same school and district can begin to create a common discourse when it comes to the process of investigating. These common terms and instances can then serve as a basis to create a greater consistency for the team and also a greater understanding of common protocol. Likewise, families, teachers, and students can also start to recognize this language in the hopes of establishing a fair and equitable system.

Subjectivity Is Limited

There will always be traces of subjectivity when processing discipline. Every situation has its own circumstances. However, with the interview component, the facts come from witnesses, not conjecture.

The Administrator Can Feel Confident of the Process

When multiple perspectives come into play, the truth is better assimilated, and therefore the investigator relies more on those common truths rather than on opinion. Conducting a comprehensive investigation not only finds the truth but also maintains the investigator's credibility and integrity.

Parents Have a Visible Blueprint of a Process

There is nothing worse than receiving an ominous call at work hearing that your child is in trouble at school. A parent's first instinct is to defend and protect. Common threads will allow a parent to see the progression of each incident with nonbiased accuracy from witnesses and their child's own account of what transpired.

Common Threads Does Not Have to Be Used for Just Discipline

School administrators will be faced with many difficult scenarios and situations that could lend themselves to using the common threads model. Teacher investigations, parent incidents, colleague-to-colleague struggles, and day-to-day fact finding can be completed more efficient by incorporating common threads.

SUMMATION

Given that people are asked to coexist in a society, disagreement will be a reality. As administrators, we must deal with the incidents as they occur; however, the real key is to deal with the individual as an ongoing process. With this philosophy, we are more likely to make a sustained, positive impact on a person's life.

There is always a victim with discipline. Be it the actual victim, the child in question, other personnel, or even the loss of instructional time, on some level discipline causes a disruption to our educational system. We must strive to ensure that we communicate a value to our system and that we have respect for our position and the actions we must take to ensure a maximized learning environment.

In order to attain that delicate balance between the individual and the collective, we must fortify our ability to handle investigations with consistency. The common threads model creates that equilibrium by establishing a methodology for investigations grounded in qualitative research. In realizing our goal of creating a safe and sound environment for learning for all children, we must limit our bias and build upon a process that establishes a systematic protocol for all investigators one incident at a time.

IV
CASE STUDIES

The following are situations that connect to each chapter. They are designed to spur on conversation and look to examine the key points of each chapter. Oftentimes, the case study is best when used prior to reading the chapter.

MUTUALLY COMBATIVE

Dr. Thomas has a problem. As the new assistant principal of Hover Middle School, he has just dealt with a fight. It seems that two girls were separated by a staff member, who stated that they were "attacking each other in the hallway." However, no one was there to witness the event. In addition, girl number 1 stated that she was "being attacked" by girl number 2.

> If you were Dr. Thomas, how would you proceed with this situation? What does "mutually combative" mean? What steps would you take to ensure a resolution? Be sure to list your action steps in answering these questions.

Action Planning

Although the administrator cannot determine if this was a fight or an attack, he or she can be fairly sure that something physical happened. It would be critical in this situation to retain the incident reports. Simply taking the word of the adult would be a mistake, as each story needs to be heard. Once secured, it would be easier to make a determination if both girls were engaged in the skirmish or if this was an attack of some sort. At that time, the principal will be able to determine the proper outcomes: parental contact, police involvement, suspensions, guidance referrals, and so forth.

Future Planning

Although helpful to determine why the event took place, the reasons behind the altercation cannot replace a consequence. In other words, the event happened. It is beneficial for the future to understand why it happened; however, administrators cannot dismiss the event due to prior circumstances.

CONFIDENTIAL MATTERS

Mr. Miller, father of Abby Miller, is really upset. To make a long story short, his daughter had been receiving threatening e-mails from an anonymous site during the school day. Although Ms. Deere, the principal, was able to investigate, identify, and levy consequences to the girls who were responsible, Mr. Miller wants to know the specific names of the girls, as he feels his daughter's safety is at risk.

If you were Ms. Deere, would you tell Mr. Miller? Why or why not?

Action Planning

By law (Family Educational Rights and Privacy Act, or FERPA), a principal is not permitted to share confidential information concerning other students. However, there are some circumstances where it would be necessary to inform a student or family of certain events or people involved in those activities. In the case of a threat, it would be reasonable to share the names of the girls (not necessarily the consequences) with Mr. Miller, as his daughter's safety was threatened.

Future Planning

Bullying is a hot topic in schools. The more proactive an administrator can be the less bullying will exist. With all instances of bullying, there should be time for conflict resolution and critical discussion between students and families. Communication builds compassion and understanding.

TIMING

Silvia, an eleventh-grade student, came to see Dr. Joyce, an assistant principal at Grady High School. Crying, Silva explained that she was teased by several other students for weeks but was nervous to tell someone about it. Finally finding her courage, she described the events that had occurred. After hearing the statements, Dr. Joyce indicated that she was not able to do anything because the incidents happened weeks ago. Dr. Joyce did her best to console Silvia and asked her to come and see her immediately if another occurrence happened.

> Do you agree with Dr. Joyce's decision? Why or why not. Please explain how you would handle the situation if you disagree.

Action Planning

There is no statute of limitation in schools, especially when it comes to bullying. Dr. Joyce should follow the common threads methodology to secure exactly what happened. To dismiss these events because of elapsed time should not be an option when it comes to the health, welfare, and safety of students.

Future Planning

Perhaps Dr. Joyce would fail to find factual information to support Silvia's claim; however, failure to respond sends a very different message to her and her family. If nothing occurred, at least the investigation was made; if something did happen, the principal can decide on appropriate actions following the event. The key is to work hard to secure each child's sense of safety in the school environment.

JUST THE FACTS

Mrs. Kline, a seventh-grade teacher, has written a referral for Gregory, a student in her class. Mrs. Kline is accusing Gregory of being insubordinate in class today; yet, on the referral, there are several incidents being described that occurred over the course of several weeks. The only incident being described today was Gregory's flipping a book to his friend.

> If you were the principal, how would you respond to this situation? Can Mrs. Kline apply past history to incriminate Gregory for present incidents?

Action Planning

If Mrs. Kline was having a problem with Gregory's behavior, she should have brought it to your attention sooner. Consequences should be progressive. Although you can investigate and levy a consequence for Gregory's behavior today, it would be difficult to include past episodes.

Future Planning

It would be a good idea to converse with Mrs. Kline to establish a protocol (phone calls to parents, conferences, etc.) for handling small incidents prior to them becoming bigger ones. (It is not being suggested that Gregory was insubordinate in the past, only that levying disciplinary measures on prior actions creates a sense of imbalance to students and families.) Now, if Mrs. Kline had been proactive and kept the principal in the loop prior to today, then perhaps a more severe consequence could be administered.

THE CONFESSION

Mr. Pierce, an assistant principal at Shady Tree High School, just wrapped up a quick discipline situation. The reason the investigation was so swift was due to the student's (Donald) confession. Mr. Pierce spoke to Donald, assigned a consequence, and called Donald's mother to inform her of the situation. Once off the phone with Donald's mother, Mr. Pierce went about his day.

> Should Mr. Pierce have investigated the situation even if he received a confession from Donald? What events could occur that would call his methods (or lack thereof) into question?

Action Planning

Mr. Pierce should have followed the common threads methodology. Allowing Donald's confession to be the only piece of evidence was a mistake. As so often occurs, students can and do change their story once they have had time to reflect and realize the severity of the incident. By not having any other evidence, Mr. Pierce is left to the mercy of Donald's opinion.

Future Planning

Often there are times when students will confess to a situation; however, even confessions should be charted on the grid sheets. This way, you can be assured that the student is telling the truth and not just assuming responsibility for someone else's actions. Likewise, the investigation could thwart the accusation that Donald was "intimidated" by Mr. Pierce and confessed under duress.

"ARE YOU CALLING MY KID A LIAR?"

Terrance Governs, an elementary principal, just had an interesting conversation with a parent. During the course of an investigation, Terrance had determined that Bobby, the parent's son, was not telling the truth about a situation. Although Terrance felt that he had the evidence to support the claim, he did not have a system to explain his methods. The parent, believing his son, had asked Terrance to defend his decision. Although Terrance explained the manner in which he handled the investigation, the parent was still not satisfied.

> How could Terrance strengthen his position with the parent? Should you ever call a student a liar?

Action Planning

Terrance could have strengthened his position by using the grid sheet. By following the process and showing the matrix (not student names but statements), one can allow the data to speak the truth rather than having to call a child a liar. Likewise, using the process gives credence to the accusations that can and do occur after data has been collected and interpreted.

Future Planning

There will be occasions when it is necessary to state that you felt a student did not tell the truth; however, be sure to make the statements about the behavior ("In this instance, I believe it is reasonable to assume Bobby lied") versus the person ("Bobby is a liar"). The more objective an administrator can be, the stronger the evidence will be in determining the next steps.

"I AM GOING TO YOUR BOSS"

The assistant principal, Dr. Janice Mayo, was conversing with Mr. Jones, a parent of a student who was just suspended for three days for stealing. Dr. Mayo was accustomed to talking with parents and always tried to be an advocate for students, even when they made mistakes. However, Mr. Jones was not interested in her pleasantries and demanded that she reverse her decision (as he claimed his son was only "fooling around" and had planned to put the cell phone back) or he would go to her boss.

> If you were Dr. Mayo, how would you respond to someone saying they were going to your boss? What steps would you take to address this situation?

Action Planning

Unfortunately, there will be times when people will go to your boss. The key to any situation is to be proactive. If possible, perhaps suggest a cooling-down period or even a second conversation later in the day. However, if the parent insists on going to see your boss, be sure to contact your boss first. Send the grid sheets to your boss. Be sure to document all that has been done. By following the process, you have the justification for your decision and a way to explain your thinking.

Future Planning

Obviously, the best case is for the principal to handle the parent situation in the building. However, one cannot assume something was wrong or actions occurred with malice because someone wants to take the claim to a higher authority. Hopefully, by following common threads, an administrator can diminish the occurrences.

THE DOUBLE WHACK

Mr. Loir, a good-hearted eleventh-grade English teacher, has just brought two boys into the office. He is accusing the boys of cheating on their final exam. Mr. Loir believes this is a serious offense and would like to give the students a zero for the grade along with the appropriate discipline.

> If you were the assistant principal, how would you handle this situation?
> If you determined the students were indeed cheating, should they be given a zero and a suspension?

Action Planning

Cheating is an intense issue in schools. Teachers can sometimes take cheating as sign of personal disrespect from a student. Using the system, if the students were not cheating, the principal would need to display the evidence (grid sheet) to Mr. Loir. If they were cheating, one would need to follow the school's policy on cheating and administer the consequences accordingly.

Future Planning

Whether or not a student should be punished twice is at the discretion of the school and community. As a rule, though, punishment should fit the crime. If a student receives a zero for the assignment, that would seem to be punishment enough. In looking toward the future, the principal would most certainly contact the parents and entertain some sort of counseling and discussion if it was deemed necessary.

TEACHER INVESTIGATION

Jennifer Grace is a good teacher. She has been a fixture in Hills Elementary School for two decades and has always done right by children and families. One day, Ms. Hamburg, a vocal parent who has a third-grade daughter, showed up at the principal's office demanding that Mrs. Grace be terminated. Ms. Hamburg accused Mrs. Grace of hitting her daughter and stated that she would "go to the newspapers" if justice was not performed.

> If you were the principal, discuss the steps you would take to solve this situation.

Action Planning

First, the principal would want to assure all parties that the matter would be taken seriously. Just because Mrs. Grace has a positive reputation does not mean she is innocent. Next, a thorough investigation must follow. Prior to rendering a decision, you may want to consult your immediate supervisor and human resources director, as there may be existing protocol that needs to be followed when investigations involve teachers.

Future Planning

The common threads method works with all types of investigations. The key is to stay calm and follow the process to secure the best attempt at truth. Obviously, if a teacher had struck a child, other personnel would be involved. Likewise, if one discovers this story was fabricated, that would also bring consequences. In addition, if one knows the parent can tend to be loud, planning when and how to inform the parent will be a critical step in what must be considered.

BUS VIDEO

Anne Moyer, mother of Daniel, is very angry. Daniel is being accused of bullying on the bus. Mrs. Moyer, who is not a typically hostile parent, wants to see the bus video because she feels her son is being "set up" by his friends. As the principal, you are aware that the video has captured Daniel in the act of bullying; however, the video has also recorded a second boy throwing papers out the window.

> If you were the principal, would you show Mrs. Moyer the video, thus confirming the initial incident? If so, what would be the ramifications? If not, how would you prove your point?

Action Planning

This is not an easy situation. A principal can certainly use the FERPA law to protect another child's identity and not show the video. Yet, seeing is believing. The correct answer is to not show the video and use the investigative evidence to make the argument, but . . .

Future Planning

Remember, art imitates life. The video only captured what has already occurred. A solid investigation can lead to the same results if planned accordingly. If there was the option of blurring out the faces of the other students, you could possibly show the video. However, do you want the parents to think there is bullying and littering occurring on the bus?

THREAT

Mrs. Wilson has just phoned the school in a panic. She indicated that her tenth-grade son Josh, who skipped school today, was distraught, angry, and intended to hurt another student because of a situation with a girl. As the principal, you have taken the call and are now faced with the decision.

> What will you do? What type of investigative plan will you use? When will it begin? Who should be involved?

Action Planning

First and foremost, the health, welfare, and safety of the students are critical. If one was unsure of the severity of the threat, the first action may be to call the authorities and possibly put the building into lockdown. Although it may seem extreme, without knowing what Josh is capable of doing, one must take every precaution. Once under control, an investigation, counseling, and potential consequences would be established for Josh depending on the details.

Future Planning

Never doubt the first instinct to secure safety. Too often principals worry about perception rather than siding with caution. If it feels wrong, it probably is. Practicing lockdown drills and having plans for these types of situations are critical components to ensuring a safe educational environment.

THE AUTHORITY

Chip French, a solid seventh-grade teacher, was having a conversation with the principal of Harvey Middle School, Mr. Joe Preston. Mr. Preston, who had just completed an investigation, was relaying the results to Chip. Mr. Preston explained to Chip that although he had given testimony to this particular situation, the facts did not match his account, and therefore, Mr. Preston was not able to suspend the child. Chip, who felt Mr. Preston was diminishing his authority, stated, "Shouldn't an adult's account receive more weight in an investigation?"

> If you were Mr. Preston, how would you respond? Should an adult's account receive more weight in an investigation?

Action Planning

Adults do receive a bit more credence when it comes to discrepancies within an investigation. However, if the investigator has no reason to believe that others are lying, and the adult's account does not match the accounts of many others, one would have to side with the facts of the case. Remember, the facts are the facts. Utilizing a consistent approach and having clear communication will not make everyone happy with each decision but will solidify the process for securing an unbiased end.

Future Planning

There will be times when a principal's decisions are unpopular. If every investigation is an opportunity for discovery, then one must allow the process, not necessarily the people involved, to dictate the end results.

THE POSSIBLE FIGHT

Amanda Reading and Allison Kline were having a good argument. Although they used to be friends, their behavior toward each other had been questionable at best. Both of their friends reported to the office that Amanda and Allison were actually going to fight after school at the old gym.

If you were the principal, what would you do? What if the girls denied the alleged fight? What is your obligation?

Action Planning

Health, welfare, and safety are paramount in any school situation. If a principal learns that a fight might occur, he or she must take the time to investigate and inform all parties involved. Even if the girls deny the incident, the principal should still investigate and discuss the subject with the girls and inform their parents. Possible courses of action could include asking parents to pick students up after school.

Future Planning

Even if an investigation does not yield an offense, it yields information. That information could be critical in dealing with the next event. Sharing the results with families opens the lines of discussion and gives all a chance to be heard.

Scenario 1

One of the greatest times of the day in middle school is dismissal. As students file out of the building, smiling and recapping the events of the day, principals can usually stand with a smile, saying goodbye, watching yet another day coming to a close. Such was the scene on this ordinary Thursday in December. Then, without warning, a teacher came into the office with two seventh-grade girls in tow. "You sit there; you sit there," he stated as he seated the obviously upset girls, separating them with three empty seats between them. "They had a fight. I'm not sure what happened. I'm just delivering them from Mrs. Richards," he exclaimed as he walked out, rightfully leaving me to deal with the incident. I stood dumbfounded, my peaceful Thursday afternoon now a little less peaceful, left to deal with an end-of-the-day incident that demanded immediate attention. Let the process begin.

After making sure that there were no injuries from this supposed "fight," I realized that there was no way I was going to be able to fully investigate this situation with literally minutes left in the school day. I asked the girls (separately) to fill out the incident report (IR) sheet to get their accounts of what had happened in class on paper. Both alluded to a scuffle that had ensued due to verbal interaction and "light pushes" that had been exchanged. The overwhelming consensus inferred that the teacher had overreacted by calling the melee a "fight."

I told both girls that I would be investigating the situation the next morning and sent them home on their respective buses. I reminded both girls to inform their parents of what had happened during last period today. I also called the girls' parents and left messages saying that the girls were involved in an incident at the end of the school day and an investigation would be conducted the following day.

A few minutes later, the classroom teacher dropped by and wanted to follow up with me concerning the incident and verbally gave me an account of what happened. "I had the class in a long line to mark their papers at the end of the period. I heard one of the girls yell loudly and looked up. Britney hit Rachel hard in the back. Then Rachel hit Britney so hard that she flew back into several other students. So I asked Mr. Thomas to bring them up to the office because I was still teaching at that point." I asked the teacher to fill out an incident report sheet. She did so, and my investigation was ready to roll, bright and early on Friday.

STEP 1: TAP YOUR RESOURCES

Friday morning settled in as only Friday mornings can in a middle school. When the daily dust settled, my investigation was on track and ready to go. I took the names of the four witnesses listed by the girls and the classroom teacher and called them to the office to fill out the incident report sheets. I had our guidance counselors call the students to the office.

Each student was given the same introductory explanation. "Good morning. The reason I'm calling you into the office today is that you were listed as a witness to an incident that took place yesterday during last period in math class. Does that ring any bells?" Answers varied from head nods to "yes" to "oh yea! That was crazy!"

STEP 2: HANDLE INCIDENT REPORT SHEETS

I handed over the IR sheets; placed each student in a private, comfortable, confidential setting; and let them fill it out without further prompting. Each student filled out the IR sheet in its entirety. When other witnesses were mentioned, I called those witnesses up next. When the process was completed, I had a total of ten IR sheets: two sheets from the girls involved in the incident, one from the classroom teacher, and seven from various witnesses mentioned by students in the investigation.

After reading the IR sheets, I was ready to chart my findings. I brought up the template and began to list facts—and only facts. I identified each IR with a number that coincided with a number on the chart so that anonymity was protected. The results of this data collection are as follows. The following pages are the actual responses from the IR Sheets. When reading these pages, remember that what was reported was a simple incident between two girls, Britney Carlton and Rachel Johnson.

Incident Report Sheet 1

Name: Britney Carlton
1. Who was involved in the incident?
   Rachel Johnson
2. Where did the incident occur?
   Math class
3. What time did the incident occur? What period if it happened in school?
   2:46, last period
4. List any and all witnesses that can confirm what happened.
   Bill Simpson
5. What happened? Please be specific and use details. You can use the back of this page if you need more room. If you need help writing your information, please let someone know and we'll help you.
   Waiting in line for the teacher to check something some girl tried to cut in front of me. I told her to go to the end of the line. I got mocked repeatedly. Then she went to the end of the line. Rachel Johnson went to "bee-bop" me and I just snapped. I pushed her then I pushed her back.

Incident Report Sheet 2

Name: Rachel Johnson
1. Who was involved in the incident?
   Myself, Britney, Brianna, Megan Kirkman
2. Where did the incident occur?
   math

3. What time did the incident occur? What period if it happened in school?
   The incident occurred last period around 2:45
4. List any and all witnesses that can confirm what happened.
   Myself, Britney, Brianna, Megan Kirkman
5. What happened? Please be specific and use details. You can use the back of this page if you need more room. If you need help writing your information, please let someone know and we'll help you.
   First, I got in line and Britney tells someone to get in the back of the line and then my friend Megan says for fun "get to the back of the line" and then Britney punches Megan so I gave her a push, not hard, to stop it. Then Britney tells me to get to the end of the f——in line. After that, me and Brianna are like jumping around and then Britney punches me and I restrain myself. Then I pushed her

Incident Report Sheet 3

Name: Megan Kirkman
1. Who was involved in the incident?

2. Where did the incident occur?

3. What time did the incident occur? What period if it happened in school?

4. List any and all witnesses that can confirm what happened.

5. What happened? Please be specific and use details. You can use the back of this page if you need more room. If you need help writing your information, please let someone know and we'll help you.
   It all started in last period math. I'm pretty sure around 2:25. We were standing in line to get our Christmas activity sheets checked by the teacher. I was in line when I heard a disturbance behind me. Maddie Wilcox was trying to butt in front of Britney Carlton. She was yelling, "end of the line!" to Maddie. She also hit Maddie. I stepped in and told Maddie to go to the end of the line. I suppose

Britney thought I was making fun of her so she struck me. I was only trying to help her out. After I got hit, I realized Britney could handle herself so I turned around and didn't really catch anything after that. I heard a few punching noises and then Mrs. Davis sent Britney and Rachel to the office.

Incident Report Sheet 4

Name: Brianna Rolleston

1. 1. Who was involved in the incident?

2. Where did the incident occur?

3. What time did the incident occur? What period if it happened in school?

4. 4. List any and all witnesses that can confirm what happened.

5. What happened? Please be specific and use details. You can use the back of this page if you need more room. If you need help writing your information, please let someone know and we'll help you.
   The incident happened in math class, last period around 2:40. The people involved were Britney Carlton and Rachel Johnson. Witnesses were Megan Kirkman, Roberta Daniels and Natalie Cruise. What happened was Britney was really mad for no reason and Rachel, Megan and I were just talking amongst ourselves and we said, "why is she so mad?" At least I think that's what one of us said. But, after she heard that Britney punched Megan in the arm and Rachel and I said, "yo, chill . . . she didn't do anything." Then about a minute passed by and me and Rachel started dancing on the side of the line to get our papers checked. And I guess Britney got really mad because we danced so close to her, but me and Britney have always danced like that since the field trip we had. But Britney punched Rachel and Rachel then turned around and said, "Whoa! What are you doing?" But I said, "Rachel, just chill out." So Rachel chilled out a little and just pushed Britney away, and that's all the conflict that happened.

Incident Report Sheet 5

Name: Bill Simpson
1. Who was involved in the incident?
   Rachel Johnson, Britney Carlton, Megan Kirkman, Fred Tera
2. Where did the incident occur?
   Math class, last period
3. What time did the incident occur? What period if it happened in school?
   Last period, around 2:30–2:45
4. List any and all witnesses that can confirm what happened.
   Mrs. Davis, Adele McMann, Cathleen Brown
5. What happened? Please be specific and use details. You can use the back of this page if you need more room. If you need help writing your information, please let someone know and we'll help you.
   Fred Tera was picking on Britney Carlton for no reason, so Britney got upset and tipped his desk over, then Britney went to turn in a paper to the teacher (Davis) while he was in line to show her his work, and Megan Kirkman (knowing Britney was upset) laughed at her and teased her and so Britney Carlton told Megan to go to the back of the line, and Megan went away. Then Brianna Rolleston (also knowing Britney was upset) was dancing in a questionable way in front of her, and then Rachel Johnson called Britney a bitch from what somebody told me after it happened, and then the teacher said there was hitting, that somebody hit somebody else. So Britney was having a bad day and everybody just wanted to make it worse, and apparently it got kind of physical, but everything happened fast, so it was hard to see what was going on.

Incident Report Sheet 6

Name: Colleen Davis (teacher)

1. Who was involved in the incident?
   Britney Carlton, Rachel Johnson
2. Where did the incident occur?
   math

3. What time did the incident occur? What period if it happened in school?
   Around 2:45
4. 4. List any and all witnesses that can confirm what happened.
   Unknown
5. What happened? Please be specific and use details. You can use the back of this page if you need more room. If you need help writing your information, please let someone know and we'll help you.
   The class was playing a holiday math game. In line, Britney said something (apparently a curse word) and hit Rachel. Rachel and Brianna were doing the "bee-bop" to Britney. Rachel hit Britney. I asked Mr. Thomas for help. He was passing by in the hall.

Incident Report Sheet 7

Name: Adele McMann
1. Who was involved in the incident?
   Britney Carlton and Rachel Johnson
2. Where did the incident occur?
   Room 205
3. What time did the incident occur? What period if it happened in school?
   Between 2:30–2:45, math, last period
4. List any and all witnesses that can confirm what happened.
   Bill Simpson, Fred Tera
5. What happened? Please be specific and use details. You can use the back of this page if you need more room. If you need help writing your information, please let someone know and we'll help you.
   Rachel Johnson was making fun of Britney Carlton and Rachel got really close to Britney and did a dance called bee-bopping. Britney pushed Rachel away but it made a loud noise. Then Rachel pushed Britney back and knocked a bunch of people over. Mrs. Davis then made everyone sit down and sent both of them to the office.

Incident Report Sheet 8

Name: Maddie Wilcox
1. Who was involved in the incident?
   Britney Carlton and Rachel Johnson
2. Where did the incident occur?
   Math room
3. What time did the incident occur? What period if it happened in school?
   Last period at around 2:35
4. List any and all witnesses that can confirm what happened.
   Brianna Rolleston, Jen Conson
5. What happened? Please be specific and use details. You can use the back of this page if you need more room. If you need help writing your information, please let someone know and we'll help you.
   Britney Carlton punched Rachel in the back and Rachel turned around. Britney said something. Then Rachel pushed her.

Incident Report Sheet 9

Name: Cathleen Brown
1. Who was involved in the incident?
   Britney Carlton, Rachel Johnson, Brianna Rolleston
2. Where did the incident occur?
   Math class, 205
3. What time did the incident occur? What period if it happened in school?
   Last period, about 2:35.
4. List any and all witnesses that can confirm what happened.
   Bill Simpson, Megan Kirkman, Fred Tera
5. What happened? Please be specific and use details. You can use the back of this page if you need more room. If you need help writing your information, please let someone know and we'll help you.
   We were doing an activity in which we had to line up for her to check our papers. Britney Carlton was already agitated because of an argument she had with Fred Tera, a guy in our class. Brianna cut in line and Britney got really mad and told Brianna to go to the

back. Either Rachel or Brianna called her a bitch and they started to do the "bee-bop" dance around her. Britney then punched Rachel. Our teacher sent them to the office.

Incident Report Sheet 10

Name: Fred Tera
1. Who was involved in the incident?
   Britney Carlton, Rachel Johnson, maybe Brianna Rolleston
2. Where did the incident occur?
   Math Class—205
3. What time did the incident occur? What period if it happened in school?
   2:30–2:50, last period
4. List any and all witnesses that can confirm what happened.
   Bill Simpson, Megan Kirkman, Maddie Wilcox.
5. What happened? Please be specific and use details. You can use the back of this page if you need more room. If you need help writing your information, please let someone know and we'll help you.
   Well Britney was annoyed and she was in line to get her paper checked by the teacher. Adele McMann was poking her with a pencil and she was getting mad. Bill Simpson told Adele to stop and she did, but then Megan started to annoy her and Bill told her to stop. Someone also told me that Brianna Rolleston was bee-bopping and that was annoying Britney as well. Then Rachel Johnson kept cutting in front of Britney so Britney had to wait even longer to get her paper checked. She kept cutting until Britney got really mad and punched her in the back.

STEP 3: REVIEW WITH AN INTERVIEW

As each student gave me an indication that they had completed the sheet, I looked over each statement and asked for clarifying points if the statements warranted further explanation. If more information was extracted from these informal interviews, I added the data onto the sheet to expand the facts.

STEP 4: EXAMINE THE CHART

Upon seeing the accounts, I realized that I was dealing with much more than a simple incident involving two girls "lightly pushing" each other. It was interesting to see that certain details were "missing" from individual accounts, where other details were emphasized depending on what relationship the witness had with certain players involved with actions that could warrant discipline. With the information in front of me, it was now time to sort through what was fact and what was opinion or theory. With numbers assigned to each person involved, I began to chart the commonalities.

The first fact I concentrated on was the physical interaction between Britney and Rachel, specifically Britney's role in the altercation.

Incident report 1: "I pushed her then I pushed her back."

Incident report 2: "Britney punches me."

Incident report 4: "But Britney punched Rachel . . ."

Incident report 6: "In line, Britney said something (apparently a curse word) and hit Rachel."

Incident report 7: "Britney pushed Rachel away but it made a loud noise."

Incident report 8: "Britney Carlton punched Rachel in the back and Rachel turned around."

Incident report 9: "Britney then punched Rachel."

Incident report 10: "She kept cutting until Britney got really mad and punched her in the back."

I charted the facts and easily saw that eight out of the ten accounts speak to Britney physically engaging against Rachel, including Britney's own confession and the observation from Mrs. Davis, the math teacher. (Note that account 3 speaks of Britney hitting Megan and Maddie but makes no mention of striking Rachel and therefore cannot count as a written record of Britney accosting Rachel in class.) Account 5 revolves around what was done to Britney to precipitate the pushing/punching. It never mentions Britney's role as an aggressor; rather, it paints the picture of Britney as a victim. Interestingly, Bill Simpson is Britney's boyfriend. (I found this information from our guidance counselor when reviewing the evidence after I compiled the information.) Nevertheless, there is an obvious picture of Britney punching or pushing Rachel in class based on fact.

Example of common threads chart on the Britney/Rachel incident: fact 1

Student/observable behavior	Britney physically engages Rachel
1	X
2	X
3	
4	X
5	
6	X
7	X
8	X
9	X
10	X

The second fact I concentrated on was Rachel's role in the incident. I found common statements that corroborated her involvement.

Incident report 2: "So I gave her a push, not hard, to stop it. . . . Then I pushed her."
Incident report 4: "So Rachel chilled out a little and just pushed Britney away."
Incident report 6: "Rachel hit Britney."
Incident report 7: "Then Rachel pushed Britney back and knocked a bunch of people over."
Incident report 8: "Then Rachel pushed her."

Five accounts back up the fact that Rachel was involved with a physical altercation with Britney, also including an admission and a teacher account. The other five accounts either dismissed Rachel's involvement or skirted around the issue. I found out from the guidance counselor that Rachel has many friends in this math class, including many of the witnesses called for this investigation. Luckily, three of those witnesses did implicate Rachel by saying that she did in fact push Britney.

Example of common threads chart on the Britney/Rachel incident: facts 1 and 2

Student/observable behavior	Britney physically engages Rachel	Rachel physically engages Britney
1	X	
2	X	X
3		
4	X	X
5		
6	X	X
7	X	X
8	X	X
9	X	
10	X	

At this point in the investigation, the common threads that have been discovered from our witnesses present enough evidence to say that Britney and Rachel are both guilty of a scuffle or fight in class. Through investigating, the girls' first account of what had happened seems to had been minimized, most likely to downplay the implications of the consequences of a fight or scuffle in class.

However, through this process, there are more implications that have presented themselves, namely, a behavior known as "bee-bopping" and the students that participated in it. The guidance counselor reported that "bee-bopping" was the practice of two or more people surrounding a student and forcibly dancing and pushing that student, not allowing the student to leave the circle and, at times, violently shaking and pushing the student while touching him or her inappropriately. The practice was obviously known to many of the students. I looked for common threads surrounding "bee-bopping."

Incident report 1: "Rachel Johnson went to 'bee-bop' me and I just snapped."
Incident report 2: "After that, me and Brianna are like jumping . . ."
Incident report 4: "Me and Rachel started dancing . . . we danced so close to her."
Incident report 5: "Then Brianna Rolleston . . . was dancing in a questionable way in front of her."
Incident report 6: "Rachel and Brianna were doing the 'bee-bop' to Britney."
Incident report 7: "Rachel got really close to Britney and did a dance called bee-bopping."
Incident report 9: "They started to do the 'bee-bop' dance around her."

Example of common threads chart on the Britney/Rachel incident: facts 1 through 3

Student/observable behavior	Britney physically engages Rachel	Rachel physically engages Britney	Rachel and Brianna "bee-bop" Britney
1	X		X
2	X	X	X
3			
4	X	X	X
5			X
6	X	X	X
7	X	X	X
8	X	X	
9	X		X
10	X		

Harassing behavior is sometimes difficult to prove. Through this investigative process, seven of the witnesses, including Rachel, Britney, and Mrs. Davis, have documented that it indeed did happen in this math class. What is curious here is that not one student reported this behavior on its own as a behavior to be concerned about, which can be tucked away as something that may need to be dealt with at a later time when planning proactively for the future.

As each witness account was dissected for facts, I listed each fact as another column and charted how many times each fact was mentioned. It is always important to track a fact that is only mentioned once or twice to sort the importance of what facts will be used to present a case. For example, it was mentioned that a student cursed or called someone a name a few times in the accounts associated with this incident. However, when I took a closer look, here was what I found in reference to those claims.

> Incident report 2: "Then Britney tells me to get to the end of the f——in line."
> Incident report 5: "Rachel Johnson called Britney a bitch from what somebody told me after it happened."
> Incident report 6: "Britney said something (apparently a curse word)."
> Incident report 9: "Either Rachel or Brianna called her a bitch."

The four reports state that a curse was said. When looked at closely, there is only one accusation based on fact, and that is report number 2, coincidentally, Rachel's account. Not one other witness recalled Britney telling Rachel to "get to the end of the f——in line." Therefore, it would be Rachel's word against Britney's and impossible to prove. The other statements elude to someone calling someone else a bitch. The wording from the IRs states, "from what somebody told me" (this witness doesn't know if it happened or not), "apparently a curse word" (speculated, so it cannot be proven), and "either Rachel or Brianna" (the witness cannot identify who said the word). From these accounts, the cursing is a nonissue as it cannot be proven or supported by fact.

STEP 5: ADDRESS THE CONSEQUENCES

After the chart had been compiled, it was time to call back the students that were identified as being involved in the incident. I called them individually from their classrooms, asking the teachers to quietly give them passes to the office. I did not announce their names over the public address system. Many students know that the investigation is commencing, so publicly embarrassing the students only builds an adversarial environment even before I speak to them.

I first presented the information to Britney. My tone was calm and supportive. As Britney saw the chart in front of her, her body language gave away that she was trying desperately to plan ahead: jittery, biting her bottom lip, and hands folded as fingers tapped subconsciously. Britney was nervous.

I explained that I used a process called "common threads" and that I interviewed a total of ten people that witnessed the event, including her teacher and herself. Using the chart, I showed Britney the facts that were in front of us.

"Britney," I said. "You were in a tough situation here. From completing this investigation, I understand that you were having a tough day and that the students in math class weren't helping. You handled it inappropriately by punching and pushing your classmates, but I want to help you get through this."

"I just snapped, Mr. Joseph. There was only so much I could take. They all knew that I was having a bad day, but they kept going and going," Britney said.

At that point, Britney had moved past the initial instinct of denial. With my redirection to acknowledge her difficulties in math class, she was more willing to discuss her actions with me. This, however, does not negate the fact that she violated the discipline code for willfully engaging in a physical confrontation with another student, or in other terms, a fight. I informed Britney that she would serve two days of suspension, as outlined in the board-approved district discipline code. She nodded her head and took the consequence well, knowing that with her own admission of physical interaction and her peers' testimony that she had no other choice than to own up to her part in the incident.

I called her parents and had them come in to pick her up to begin her suspension. They informed me that Britney had explained the story the night before and they were expecting my call sometime today.

After speaking to Britney's parents, I called in Rachel. Rachel was in tears and sat down with a thud into a chair across from my desk.

"This isn't fair. I was just defending myself against her. And all I did was push. She punched me," Rachel began. "I know I'm going to get suspended and I didn't do anything," she continued.

I responded calmly. "Rachel, I realize that you are upset with this situation and I need you to know that I took your version of the facts very seriously. I interviewed ten people, including your teacher and the witnesses you provided."

"Well, Britney's witnesses will say anything to get her off. They hate me."

"Rachel, some of the witnesses that you called verified that you pushed Britney and bee-bopped her along with Brianna. You are not innocent here," I said quietly.

"But, Mr. Joseph, she punched me and I turned around and did nothing. I could have done so much more to her, but I restrained myself and just pushed her hard. It could have been much worse. Don't you understand that?"

"Rachel, you just admitted that you willfully pushed her. That's the definition of a 'fight' in our discipline code. In addition, as you can see, I have witnesses that back that up. You will be receiving two days of suspension."

Rachel cried and held her hands to her face. "It's not fair."

I called Rachel's father, and he came to pick his daughter up from school. Both students received the appropriate discipline, and all forms were filled out to completion. When I held conferences with both sets of parents separately, I explained their daughters' roles in the situation. I was careful not to mention any of the names of the students that were involved. When speaking to Britney's mother and father, I had to refer to Rachel as "the other student," in keeping in compliance with FERPA (Family Educational Rights and Privacy Act) laws. It is against the law for me to share discipline with other families, even if the students are directly involved in that certain incident.

I called in Brianna last. She had no idea what she was doing in my office and seemed surprised that I had called her back in for this meeting. When I explained that the bee-bopping was technically harassment and that she would be receiving a warning for it, she frowned and said, "Everybody does it, Mr. Joseph."

I responded by saying that this time she was caught and that I would be addressing the practice of bee-bopping to the student body and explain the consequences, so that something like this wouldn't happen again. She received her warning and was on her way.

STEP 6: DECIDE ON FUTURE PLANNING

After informing the students and parents about the discipline, I met with the grade-level guidance counselor to discuss future planning with all involved. Work arrangements were made for the girls on suspension. Her teachers were notified that work was needed for the next two days. Details were not included to the "why" of the event. The girls' parents were informed that they could pick up the work at the end of the next day.

The guidance counselor and I discussed getting the girls together when they returned from suspension to process through why the incident happened and what can be done to prevent any further incidents. Random "check-ins" would be put into place to see if all involved in the incident have in fact put the incident behind them and moved on in a positive direction.

In addition, we talked about options to address the students about ceasing the practice of "bee-bopping" in school. We settled on a general announcement during lunch so that the entire grade could be addressed about the inappropriate nature of this type of dancing.

Hopefully, by this account of the facts that were presented, an administrator or other school official will be able to clearly explain and feel reasonably confident that a well-defined picture of the event has been systematically utilized. The common threads method is not an exact science. We are not trained detectives and do not pretend to be experts in investigations. The common threads model provides a template to sift through the speculation and get to the frequent details of the situation. The difficult decisions that have to be made when dealing with disciplinary issues can be minimized by having a better understanding of what actually happened in an incident.

SCENARIO 1

INCIDENT REPORT

The information on this incident report sheet will remain confidential.

Name: _____ Date: _____

Grade: _____ Homeroom: _____

Parents/guardians names (first and last): _____

Home phone number: _____

Other phone number(s): _____ (cell/work) _____ (cell/work)

1. Who was involved in the incident?
   _____

2. Where did the incident occur?
   _____

3. What time did the incident occur? What period if it happened in school?
   _____

4. List any and all witnesses that can confirm what happened.
   _____

5. What happened? Please be specific and use details. Only report what you directly witnessed. You can use the back of this page if you need more room. If you need help writing your information, please let someone know, and we will help you.

   _____
   _____
   _____
   _____
   _____
   _____
   _____

Scenario 2

There are little things that school administrators do to help run their schools easier. These are ideas that are usually not taught in any course or classroom and are specific to a certain culture of a school community. One of these things at Thompson High School was for the administrators to stand in the parking lot every morning and personally greet each car in the car line.

On any given morning, approximately 100 to 150 cars transported students into Thompson High. Each parent was met with a friendly smile and a wave, and the school community loved it. It gave parents a sense of safety and security to see the men and women that ran their children's school out there each day making sure their children were safe and in the best possible environment.

Even though the administrators at Thompson High had stumbled onto a highly successful "little thing" in the morning that made their lives infinitely easier, it also opened them up to the possibility of being sitting ducks for parents that wanted a captive audience of a principal. This was one of those mornings.

Mr. Bristow waved to Principal Dave as he always did in the car line. He dropped off his son and headed out of the parking lot. Out of the corner of Dave's eye, he saw Mr. Bristow pull into a visitor's parking spot and turn off his car. He got out of his car and headed to the student drop-off area where Dave and his partners (all principals of Thompson High) were greeting the constantly flowing car line.

"You have a minute?" Mr. Bristow said, hands on his hips, chest pumped out, and his head cocked to his side.

"I will in a few minutes, Mr. Bristow. Let me get all of our kids in the building safe and sound," Dave replied, continuing to wave on car after car.

"You have other people out here to do that. I need you now." Mr. Bristow crossed his arms, and Dave noticed that his chest was now heaving and his lips were pursed. This was not going to end well if Dave didn't address his issue soon.

After a few more waves at the passing cars, Dave asked his colleagues to take over the line. Dave's colleagues waved him on and got back to greeting the parents and students. Dave proceeded to his office with Mr. Bristow.

"Come on in," Dave said cheerfully. "How can I help you, Tom?"

Mr. Bristow sat down on the edge of his chair and leaned forward. "I know that you told me that you treat bullying as your number 1 issue in this school, but whatever you are doing, it's not working. I also know that if my boy is bullied by his so-called classmates one more time, I'll have every news van in the county in this office demanding answers." Tom Bristow was now on the verge of exploding.

Dave calmly said, "Tom, what's going on? What happened and who is bullying Ethan?"

Dave knew that Tom Bristow was an extremely nervous man that brought his own anxieties onto his son on a daily basis. As soon as Tom's son, Ethan, walked into the house, Tom would ask, "What happened at school today? Did anybody bother you?" Ethan would talk about his day, and his father would pick apart each minute, usually encouraging Ethan to skip through what he felt was unimportant until Tom found a topic that resembled any type of inappropriate behavior.

Once a negative incident was established, both Tom and Ethan would dissect the issue until both father and son were reeling in panic and fear. So was the cycle of incident reporting from Ethan Bristow, through his father, Tom.

"This time it's Leo Zimmer. He threatened Ethan's life and property. I want him arrested and thrown into an alternative school. And if he gets a slap on the wrist, I'll be on the phone with your superintendent faster than you can try to make excuses. You see? I have his number in my speed dial."

"I understand, Tom. Let's start from the beginning." Dave knew that his superintendent published his personal cell phone on our district's web page, so he wasn't too concerned about the empty phone call threat. He also had these conversations with Tom on a biweekly basis. He let Tom explain that Leo was friends with the bunch of kids that continually harassed Ethan, and he knew this was a retribution strike against Ethan for trying to get the bullying behavior to stop. Tom's conspiracy theories usually amounted to circumstantial nonsense, but Dave always listened to Tom because (1) Tom needed to have an ear to exhaust his anxieties for his son, and (2), there may be some evidence that Tom spoke about that was needed to process the impending investigation of bullying against Ethan Bristow.

Tom went on to say that in art class, Leo allegedly told Ethan that he would "beat his damn ass" and that he would break his three-dimensional airplane model that Ethan was building in art class. Much of the story was drenched in opinion and Tom's dramatic flourishes. In addition, he claimed that Leo's verbal attacks were commenced without reason or provocation, which was another aspect of Tom's stories that was consistent, although not always true.

Dave let Tom go through the entire story, emotions intact. Tom seemed exhausted after he was finished. Dave remembered that when it comes to being a parent, nothing is as important as the safety of that parent's child.

Dave waited a few seconds to make sure that Tom was completely finished with his story and said, "Listen, Tom. We will start investigating today, and we'll make sure Ethan is safe. I can never promise that Ethan will not be bullied. We do everything we can to prevent it, but the reality is that bullying will always be an issue in schools. What I can promise is that we will do everything in our power, and the discipline code's reach, to make sure it doesn't happen again. I will call you when we have some answers, and I'll keep you in the loop. Thanks for trusting me with the issue. Okay?"

Tom shook his head slowly and stood up. He extended his hand and said, "Thanks, Mr. Nolan. It's my boy, you know?"

"Yes, I do." Dave said and shook Tom's hand. Tom headed out the door, and Dave got to work.

Dave grabbed his incident report sheets and gathered his team. Dave first called upon Ethan Bristow to get his side of the story. Ethan's father would sometimes stretch the truth to fit his own paranoid version of high school drama, and the first thing that had to be done was to hear exactly what happened from the horse's mouth.

Ethan came into Dave's office and sat respectfully in the chair across from Dave. The chairs were in front of Dave's desk, to create an even playing field. There was no fear of power moves or manipulation with Mr. Nolan. He was a good guy.

"Hey, Ethan!" Dave said cheerfully. "I heard from your dad this morning. What's going on at lunch?" Ethan shifted in his seat a bit. His dad had once again violated his trust by running to Mr. Nolan. "It's not that big of a deal, Mr. Nolan. Just stupid drama from the frat boys."

The frat boys were the group of kids that thought they owned the school. They were the cool kids. The popular clique. The ones who made your life miserable if you dared to look at them the wrong way. They were textbook definitions of bullies. And they were good at it.

Ethan went on to explain that he was "friends" with some of the frat boys, and they were fine with him, too, as long as Leo wasn't around. Once Leo surfaced in the group, they turned on him quickly, and it could be merciless.

"I was eating with my friends and had to get up to go to throw out my trash. I guess that's when Leo saw his chance. Out of the corner of my eye, I watched him move into my spot and spread his stuff out." Ethan was very matter of fact about his recounting of the lunchroom scene.

"I came back from the bathroom and stood behind Leo, obviously wanting my seat back. Leo pretended I wasn't there for the first few seconds until the rest of the guys noticed I was standing there and kept looking at me. He didn't even turn around. He just said, 'If you touch me, I'm going to beat your darn ass and I'm going to do it in front of your dad.' I kept standing there and said, 'No, you're not.' He turned to me and said, 'You wanna bet?' I looked back and said, 'No, I don't bet.' Then he turned around and kept talking to the guys and ignored me."

"Did you ever get your seat back?" Dave asked.

"No . . . it was close to the end of the period so I just walked away," Ethan replied with his head down.

"So what happened next?" Dave inquired.

"In art class, Leo got into my business again and told me that he was going to break my 3-D airplane model that I've been building. I told him, 'No, you won't,' and he stared at me smiling. John can verify that for you. He saw the whole thing."

"Is John a friend of yours or Leo's?" Dave asked.

"Depends upon the day," Ethan retorted. "If Leo's not around we're fine. If he's there, he hates me. Whatever."

Dave put down his pen and paper and looked Ethan in the eye. "Ethan, why do you hang out with these guys?"

A few seconds went by, and Leo quietly answered. "They're my friends. I don't know. No one should be able to tell me who I like to hang out with. They're all cool with me until Leo comes around. I'm not afraid of him. He'd never touch me. I'm bigger than him. I just tell my dad all of this stuff because he keeps asking and asking. And then when I do he just . . . you know; he flips out and snitches on me."

"Well, buddy," Dave picked up his pen. "What you are describing to me is against our discipline code, and Leo cannot do it. He knows it. You know it. Your dad is simply looking out for you. Let me get some witnesses. I'll keep your name out of it as always."

"It's the regular people, Mr. Nolan. You know them. And they always know it's me . . . or my dad," Ethan said dejectedly.

"Either way, I'm keeping your name confidential." Dave handed Ethan a pass back to class. "Have a good day, bud. Stay away from the drama, okay?"

"Sure, Mr. Nolan. Thanks." Ethan walked out of the office to face the day.

Dave and his team called up Ethan's friends one by one and took their statements. He had them fill out incident report sheets and questioned them about the events of the lunchroom and art class. The guys had been through this before, and they knew better than to try and lie or distort the truth. Mr. Nolan always found a way to sift through the "I don't know" and "I didn't see anything."

Incident Report Sheet 1

Name: Ethan Bristow

1. Who was involved in the incident?
   Leo Zimmer
2. Where did the incident occur?
   Lunch and Art
3. What time did the incident occur? What period if it happened in school?
   Lunch Time and 7th period art class
4. List any and all witnesses that can confirm what happened.
   Myself, Trevor Washington, Rob Stancatto, John Powell, Ben Ready, and Sam Torren
5. What happened? Please be specific and use details. You can use the back of this page if you need more room. If you need help writing your information, please let someone know and we'll help you.
   On Monday, 3/11/13, at the lunch table, Leo Zimmer told me that Trevor Washington texted him, and told him that I got Trevor suspended. Then, at lunch, I was sitting next to Leo. I got up to throw something away, went back to the table, and was getting ready to sit down in my seat, which Leo had moved into, between me and Rob Stancatto, when Leo said to me, "If you touch me I'm going to beat your damn ass." I sat down without pushing or touching Leo intentionally, and Leo then said to me, "I'm going to beat you up in front of your dad, too." I said, "No, you're not." Leo responded then by saying, "How much do you want to bet?" I replied by saying, "I don't bet." Leo didn't say anything to me for the rest of the lunch period. In art, I got up from my seat to get an eraser from the art cart. Leo went to get something at the cart, too, and told me, "I'm going to break up your plane, too." I said, "No, you're not." John Powell may have heard Leo say this to me, because after I mentioned the plane, he looked up and smiled. John knew that I flew remote control airplanes because John saw me flying a remote controlled plane at the park one day

Incident Report Sheet 2

Name: Trevor Washington
1. Who was involved in the incident?
   I think Ethan and Leo
2. Where did the incident occur?
   Lunch
3. What time did the incident occur? What period if it happened in school?
   Lunch Time
4. List any and all witnesses that can confirm what happened.
   Not sure
5. What happened? Please be specific and use details. You can use the back of this page if you need more room. If you need help writing your information, please let someone know and we'll help you.
   Ethan and Leo were arguing about something, as usual. I got suspended for bullying Ethan, which I really didn't do, so I stay out of everything. Ethan never stops and no one likes him at our table.

Incident Report Sheet 3

Name: Rob Stancatto
1. Who was involved in the incident?
   Ethan and Leo
2. Where did the incident occur?
   Lunch
3. What time did the incident occur? What period if it happened in school?
   Lunch Time
4. List any and all witnesses that can confirm what happened.
   Ethan, Leo, John, and maybe Ben
5. What happened? Please be specific and use details. You can use the back of this page if you need more room. If you need help writing your information, please let someone know and we'll help you.
   Leo told Ethan to leave the table because no one likes him. I didn't hear anybody say anything about beating anybody up. Ethan asks

me to save his seat when Ethan gets up, and Leo takes Ethan's seat. Ethan asks Leo why he does that, but never calls him names. Leo tells him to leave the table every time.

Incident Report Sheet 4

Name: John Powell
1. Who was involved in the incident?
   Ethan and Leo
2. 2. Where did the incident occur?
   Lunch
3. What time did the incident occur? What period if it happened in school?
   Lunch Time
4. List any and all witnesses that can confirm what happened.
   Ethan, Leo
5. What happened? Please be specific and use details. You can use the back of this page if you need more room. If you need help writing your information, please let someone know and we'll help you.
   Leo took Ethan's seat, but I don't know what was said after that. A few minutes before Leo took Ethan's seat, Leo asked Ethan why he was sitting there.

Incident Report Sheet 5

Name: Ben Ready
1. Who was involved in the incident?
   Ethan and Leo
2. Where did the incident occur?
   Lunch
3. What time did the incident occur? What period if it happened in school?
   Lunch Time
4. List any and all witnesses that can confirm what happened.
   Ethan, Leo
5. What happened? Please be specific and use details. You can use the back of this page if you need more room. If you need help writing your information, please let someone know and we'll help you.

Leo asked Ethan why he was sitting at the table because Leo didn't like him. There could have been something else that was said but I didn't hear it. When Ethan came back to his seat, Leo said that he would beat him up. Ethan said that he heard Leo say the word "ass." I didn't listen to what was said after that.

Incident Report Sheet 6

Name: Sam Torren
1. Who was involved in the incident?
   Leo Zimmer
2. Where did the incident occur?
   Lunch
3. What time did the incident occur? What period if it happened in school?
   Lunch
4. List any and all witnesses that can confirm what happened.
   Don't' know any
5. What happened? Please be specific and use details. You can use the back of this page if you need more room. If you need help writing your information, please let someone know and we'll help you.
   Me and Leo are cousins so I need this to stay quiet PLEASE. Ethan got up to throw something away. Leo moved over to say something to another kid. Ethan came back to sit down and asked Leo to move. Then Leo said, "Touch me and I'll beat your damn ass." Then Leo said, "Let's go into the bathroom and fight," and Leo stood up, but Ethan didn't, then Leo sat down.

Incident Report Sheet 7

Name: Reid Diamond
1. Who was involved in the incident?
   Leo Zimmer
2. Where did the incident occur?
   Art
3. What time did the incident occur? What period if it happened in school?
   7th period art class

4. List any and all witnesses that can confirm what happened.
   Leo and Ethan
5. What happened? Please be specific and use details. You can use the back of this page if you need more room. If you need help writing your information, please let someone know and we'll help you.
   Leo did say to Ethan that he would break his model plane.

Incident Report Sheet 8

Name: Leo Zimmer
1. Who was involved in the incident?
   Leo Zimmer and Ethan Bristow
2. Where did the incident occur?
   Lunch and Art Class
3. What time did the incident occur? What period if it happened in school?
   Lunch and Period 7
4. List any and all witnesses that can confirm what happened.
   Ethan, Ben Ready
5. What happened? Please be specific and use details. You can use the back of this page if you need more room. If you need help writing your information, please let someone know and we'll help you.
   I was messing with Ethan. I said I would beat him up and break his plane. I am sorry.

Common Threads Investigation Report

Date of Incident: Tuesday, 3/12/13
Alleged Offender(s): Leo Zimmer
Alleged Victim(s): Ethan Bristow
Alleged Offense(s): Leo Zimmer told Ethan Bristow that he would "beat his damn ass." Leo told Ethan that he would break his 3-D airplane model from art class.

Conclusion

Leo is guilty of committing both offenses.

Student/ Observable Behavior	At lunch, Leo told Ethan "If you touch me, I'll beat your damn ass."	At lunch, Leo told Ethan "I'm going to beat you up in front of your dad, too."	In art class, Leo told Ethan that he would break Connor's remote-controlled airplane.
Ethan Bristow	Y	Y	Y
Trevor Washington			
Rob Stancatto	?	?	
John Powell	?	?	
Ben Ready	Y	?	
Sam Torren	Y	?	
Reid Diamond			Y
Leo Zimmer	Y	Y	Y

Rationale

After at first denying the accusations, Leo admitted to committing all the reported offenses. Students witnessed Leo commit each offense as reported.

Notes

1. 3/13/13 conversation with Ethan Bristow. Ethan said that
   - On Monday, 3/11/13, at the lunch table, Leo Bristow told him that Trevor Washington texted Leo and told him that Ethan got Trevor suspended.
   - On Tuesday, 3/12/13, at the lunch table:
     - Ethan was sitting next to Leo Zimmer. Ethan got up to throw something away, went back to the table, and was getting ready to sit down in his seat, which Leo had moved into, between Ethan and another student (Rob Stancatto), when Leo said to him, "If you touch me I'm going to beat your damn ass." Leo sat down without pushing or touching Leo intentionally, and Leo then said to him, "I'm going to beat you up in front of your dad, too." Ethan said, "No, you're not." Leo responded then by saying, "How much do you want to bet?" Leo replied by saying, "I don't bet." Leo didn't say anything to Ethan for the rest of the lunch period.

- Ethan said that the following students were sitting at the lunch table when this occurred: Rob Stancatto, John Powell, Ben Ready, and Sam Torren.
- On Tuesday, 3/12/13 in Mrs. Fuimano's art class:
  - Ethan got up from his seat to get an eraser from the art cart. Leo went to get something at the cart, too, and told Ethan, "I'm going to break up your plane, too." Ethan said, "No, you're not."
  - Ethan said that John Powell may have heard Leo say this to Ethan, because after Ethan mentioned the plane, he looked up and smiled.
  - Ethan said that John knew that Ethan flew remote-control airplanes because John saw him flying a remote-controlled plane at the park one day.
2. 3/13/13 conversation with Rob Stancatto about lunch on Tuesday, 3/13/13
    - Leo told Ethan to leave the table because no one likes him.
    - He didn't hear anybody say anything about beating anybody up.
    - Ethan asks Rob to save his seat when Ethan gets up, and Leo takes Ethan's seat. Ethan asks Leo why he does that but never calls him names. Leo tells him to leave the table.
3. 3/13/13 conversation with John Powell about lunch on 3/13/13
    - Leo took Ethan's seat, but John said that he doesn't know what was said after that.
    - A few minutes before Leo took Ethan's seat, Leo asked Ethan why he was sitting there.
4. 3/13/13 conversation with Ben Ready about lunch on 3/13/13
    - Leo asked Ethan why he was sitting at the table because Leo didn't like him. He said that there could have been something else that was said, but he didn't hear it.
    - When Ethan came back to his seat, Leo said that he would beat him up. Ethan said that he heard Leo say the word "ass." He didn't listen to what was said after that.
5. 3/13/13 conversation with Sam Torren about lunch on 3/13/13
    - He and Leo are cousins.
    - Ethan got up to throw something away. Leo moved over to say something to another kid. Ethan came back to sit down and asked Leo to move. Then Leo said, "Touch me and I'll beat your damn

ass." Then Leo said let's go into the bathroom and fight and Leo stood up, but Ethan didn't; then Leo sat down.
6. 3/13/13 conversation with Reid Diamond
   - Reid said that Leo did say to Ethan that he would break his model plane.

Closure

Dave called Mr. Bristow and explained that his team's investigation was completed.

"Did that kid get expelled for bullying my son?" he asked.

"I can't share that, Mr. Bristow. As you know there are laws that prevent me from doing so, but I can assure you that we followed our district's discipline code to the letter of the law," Dave said calmly.

"Probably got a slap on the hand. That's usually code for 'you didn't do anything.'" Mr. Bristow dryly mumbled.

"That's not the case, Mr. Bristow," Dave said. "Just let me know if Ethan runs into any more issues, and I'll be here for you."

"Thanks for the call. I'm sure I'll be talking to you again," Mr. Bristow said as he hung up the phone.

Mr. Bristow had no idea how much work went into the investigation on Ethan's claims that he was bullied by Leo Zimmer. He also had no idea how methodically the facts were studied to reach a conclusion and to get Leo to admit to his participation in a bullying issue. However, Dave's primary focus was for the students under his care. If parents did not totally appreciate his efforts, that was okay. He worked hard for his students and their safety.

This one was a win in Dave's book.

Bibliography

Bayko, Wilma Alice. "Building Positive School Culture: The Principal's Journey." PhD diss., University of Alberta, Canada, 2005.

Besaw, Daniel M. "An Investigation into School-wide Discipline Policies." PhD diss., Pacific Lutheran University, Tacoma, WA, 2006.

Bireda, Martha R. *Eliminating Racial Profiling in School Discipline: Cultures in Conflict*. Lanham, MD: Scarecrow, 2002.

Boyce, Seamus P. "Inadvertent Board Actions That Create Liability." *School Administrator* 66, no. 4 (2009): 34.

Bursztyn, Alberto M. *Handbook of Special Education*. Lanham, MD: Rowman & Littlefield, 2008.

Claubaugh, Gary K., and Edward G. Rozycki. *Understanding Schools: The Foundations of Education*. New York: Harper & Row, 1990.

Creswell, W. John. *Research Design: Qualitative, Quantitative and Mixed Methods Approaches*. 2nd ed. Thousand Oaks, CA: Sage, 2003.

Dake, Joseph A., James H. Price, and Susan K. Telljohann. "The Nature and Extent of Bullying at School." *Journal of School Health* 73, no. 5 (May 2003): 173–80.

Domine, Vanessa Elaine. *Rethinking Technology in Schools*. New York: Peter Lang, 2009.

Feinberg, Walter, and Jonas F. Soltis. *School and Society*. New York: Teachers College Press, 1998.

Feldman, Martha S. *Social limits to discretion: An organizational perspective*. Oxford: Oxford University Press, 1992.

Gunzelmann, Betsy. *Hidden Dangers: Subtle Signs of Failing Schools*. Lanham, MD: Rowman & Littlefield, 2007.

Hall, Edward T. *The Silent Language*. Greenwich, CT: Fawcett, 1959.

Jaeger, M. "The Use of Discretionary Authority: The Safe Schools Act, 2000, and the Faculty of St. Roy's Catholic Secondary School." Paper, Brock University, St. Catharines, Ontario, 2005.

Jeynes, William. *American Educational History: School, Society, and the Common Good.* Thousand Oaks, CA: Sage, 2007.

Katsiyannis, Antonis, and John W. Maag. "Manifestation Determination as a Golden Fleece." *Exceptional Children* 68, no. 1 (Fall 2001): 85–96.

Lane, Kenneth E., Michael D. Richardson, and Dennis W. Van Berkum, eds. *The School Safety Handbook: Taking Action for Student and Staff Protection.* Lancaster, PA: Technomic Publishing, 1996.

Marzano, Robert J. *What Works in Schools.* Alexandria, VA: ASCD, 2003.

Mason, Chad. *An Assistant Principal's Guide . . . Into the Fire: How to Prepare for and Survive the Position.* Lanham, MD: Rowman & Littlefield, 2007.

McGregor, Douglas. *The Human Side of Enterprise.* New York: McGraw-Hill, 1960.

Merriam, Sharan B. *Qualitative Research and Case Study Application in Education.* San Francisco: Jossey-Bass, 1998.

Osborne, Allan G., and Charles J. Russo. *Discipline in Special Education.* Thousand Oaks, CA: Corwin, 2009.

Richardson, Julia. "Avoidance as an Active Mode of Conflict Resolution." *Team Performance Management: An International Journal* 1, no. 4 (1995): 19–25.

Sherman, Robert R., and Rodman B. Webb. *Qualitative Research in Education: Focus and Methods.* London: Falmer, 1988.

Simpson, Marcus Todd. "The Impact of Schoolwide Positive Behavior Support on the Discipline Gap in the Middle School Setting." EdD diss., Walden University 2010.

Singleton, Glenn E., and Curtis Linton. *Courageous Conversations About Race: A Field Guide for Achieving Equity in Schools.* Thousand Oaks, CA: Corwin, 2006.

Smith, Paul R. *What Do You Do Around Here Anyway? Real-Life Discussion Generators for Wannabe Principals.* Lanham, MD: Hamilton Books, 2010.

Stevick, E. Doyle, and Bradley A. U. Levinson. *Reimagining Civic Education: How Diverse Societies Form Democratic Citizens.* Lanham, MD: Rowman & Littlefield, 2007.

StudyMode. "The Rise and Effect of Single Parent Families." June 2008. www.studymode.com/.

Sturgess, Tonya K. "Does Discipline Only Skim the Surface? The Relationship between Teachers' Races and Student Discipline in Elementary and Secondary Schools." PhD diss., Capella University, 2011.

Wanko, Michael. *Safe Schools: Crisis Prevention and Response*. Historical Dictionaries of Religions, Philosophies, and Movements. Lanham, MD: Scarecrow, 2001.

Webb, Owen D. "Student Perceptions of Discretion in Discipline: Seeking Resolution and Restoration in a Punitive Culture." Master's thesis, Brock University, St. Catharines, Ontario, 2009.

Wiseman, Alexander W. *Principals under Pressure: The Growing Crisis*. Lanham, MD: Rowman & Littlefield, 2005.

Yin, Robert K. *Case Study Research: Design and Methods*. 2nd ed. Thousand Oaks, CA: Sage, 1994.

www.ingramcontent.com/pod-product-compliance
Lightning Source LLC
Chambersburg PA
CBHW070734230426
43665CB00016B/2239